HEARTBREAK FARM

A Farmer and his Farm in Wartime

To Christine and Judith
and in memory of Ken

HEARTBREAK FARM

A FARMER AND HIS FARM IN WARTIME

FRANCES MOUNTFORD

SUTTON PUBLISHING

First published in 1997 by
Sutton Publishing Limited · Phoenix Mill
Thrupp · Stroud · Gloucestershire · GL5 2BU

British Library Cataloguing in Publication Data
A catalogue record for this book is available from the British Library

ISBN 0 7509 1390 8

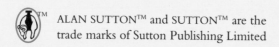
ALAN SUTTON™ and SUTTON™ are the
trade marks of Sutton Publishing Limited

Typeset in 13/18pt Garamond.
Typesetting and origination by
Sutton Publishing Limited.
Printed in Hong Kong by
Midas Printing Ltd.

Contents

ACKNOWLEDGEMENTS vii

Chapter One
THE FARM BOY 1

Chapter Two
THE TOWN WIFE 13

Chapter Three
STARTING OUT 24

Chapter Four
WORK AND WORKERS 37

Chapter Five
CAMP FARM 64

Chapter Six
VISITING EGG HILL FARM 80

Chapter Seven
WARTIME 84

Chapter Eight
THE MEN FROM THE MINISTRY 96

CONTENTS

Chapter Nine
PLOUGH THE MARSH 108

Chapter Ten
COOPED IN TOWN 121

Chapter Eleven
A VILLAGE HOME 136

Chapter Twelve
LEANING OVER THE GATE 140

BIBLIOGRAPHY 144

Acknowledgements

My grateful thanks to my husband, Alan, for advice and encouragement, to Christine Hills and Norma Rogers for memories, to Dr John Martin, De Montfort University, for kindly supplying information, and to Faber and Faber Ltd for permission to quote George Henderson.

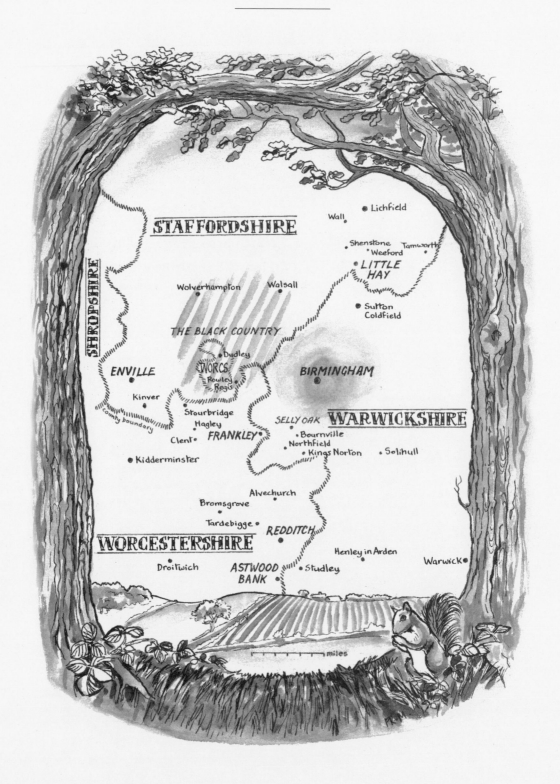

CHAPTER ONE

The Farm Boy

The baby was born on a frosty December night, thirteen days before the start of the new century, in the red brick farmhouse below Frankley Beeches.

He was given three solid Christian names, Frederick William Garibaldi, but usually he was called Ray, from the first part of his surname. Garibaldi was for his uncle Gari who had been christened at a time when the charismatic Italian general had been at the height of his popularity in England. Ray was born when families were large and this family was no exception. He was the second child of George Raybould and his vivacious wife Isabella. Their first was a girl, another Isabella, but always called Issy. Ray was followed by six brothers. By the time his last brother was born he was eighteen years old.

Ray's father, George, was a typical farmer of the period. His farm was just over a hundred acres, and, like the vast majority of farmers, he rented the property. It was an arable and grassland farm. George kept no sheep, but he had cattle, pigs, and, of course, horses, which were essential for working the land.

Everyone round the area knew Frankley Beeches, a clump of beech trees atop an airy hill, from which on a clear day seven counties could be seen, as well as, nearby, Bartley and Frankley reservoirs which were then being constructed to store Welsh water for the rapidly expanding city of Birmingham. Egg Hill Farm lay about half a mile along the lane from the Beeches and its fields ran down the hill, almost, but not quite, to the edge of the reservoirs. The land belonged to Lord Charles George Lyttleton, the 8th Viscount Cobham, who lived at Hagley Hall near the foot of the Clent Hills.

Ray, the boy, was reared to work. His few years at school were undistinguished, while his time at home was largely filled with whatever farm tasks he could manage to do for his size and age. His outings and treats were few. Visits to his Uncle Walter at Middle Park Farm, Selly Oak, just a few miles away, made a diversion. Uncle Walter carried on farming there now that Ray's grandfather was dead, and Ray and his brothers loved to go there for Middle Park was a place to visit and did not represent continual work as did their own farm.

"There was a splendid dairy there," Ray remembered. "Oh! you should have seen it! And there was a lake as well. It was a lovely place, y'know, with four towers, like a castle." Ray was fond of his Uncle Walter, who remained a bachelor, and he loved Middle Park. He never loved Egg Hill, where he was born and on which, working for his father, he expended the strength of his youth for many weary years.

Middle Park had originally been rented by his grandfather, a brick maker and a Black Country man, to accommodate some of the horses that were used to haul the brick wagons at his brick yard in Harborne.

Once upon a time there had been a photograph of this grandfather. "He had whiskers all round his chin," Ray said, "but he didn't have a moustache." Ray had been born a few years after his grandfather had died of bronchitis and so had never known him, yet remnants of Black Country speech lived on in the family, passed down from at least three generations of Black Country men who had lived in Oldbury, Netherton and Rowley Regis. "Ow bist, ower wench?" Ray would sometimes jokingly enquire, or "Let's be off wum."

Once Uncle Walter fired his gun out through Middle Park windows at a burglar but missed him. Ray never took to shooting, nor owned a shotgun, although his brothers were enthusiastic. One brother shot a buzzard at Frankley in 1934 which was presented to the Natural History Museum in Birmingham. Another buzzard had been shot at Frankley in 1898, just after his father had settled at Egg Hill. This one had been killed by his father's cousin, who farmed at nearby Frog Mill, and it was also preserved in a collection.

Ray learned to ride. "Uncle Walter taught me," he said. "I was the only one as learned to ride, the others weren't interested." He had learned on the pony, Ben, who was still grazing in the paddock at Egg Hill at the age of about thirty-five in 1940. From boyhood Ray worked with horses. They shared his long days of toil: ploughing, harrowing, harvesting; the sun, wind and rain, the lonely fields. The Shire breed was at its peak then.

When his grandfather had first moved to Middle Park in 1873 there had been no established breed of cart horse. He had bred strong draught horses to pull the brick lorries but there were no thoroughbred Shires in those days. Distinct types of heavy horse were emerging in certain areas and for particular kinds of work and gradually the breeding of heavy horses became rationalised. The Clydesdales in the north and the Suffolks in East Anglia became differentiated from the Shires across the Midland counties. Stud books were started to record the breeding which was kept true to type.

A Shire Stallion in 1910 (his weight: approximately 1 ton)

Heavy horses were often portrayed at this angle to show off the muscular hindquarters which gave them the power to draw heavy loads.

Whilst he was at Middle Park, Ray's grandfather saw the development and

A Brick Lorry.

A rambling house, gothicised to Victorian taste with castellated towers at each corner.

Middle Park Farm
Selly Oak

F.R.M.

from an old photograph

from the Northfield Rate Books : November 1875

Griffins Hill: House, Barn, Carthouse, Stables, Loft
Cowhouses, Yard, Garden, Land and Premises.
          M. F. Raybould   occupier
          M. V. Ledsam   owner
118 acres. 2 roods. 12 perches
Gross estimated rental.......£360

EGG HILL FARM
FRANKLEY
WORCESTERSHIRE

Church tower was built with stone from Manor House, (home of Lyttletons), which was burned down in the Civil War to prevent Cromwell's soldiers from occupying it.

ST. LEONARD'S CHURCH.

GEORGE EDWARD RAYBOULD at EGG HILL 1897 to 1949
Landlord: Viscount Cobham (Lyttleton family), Hagley Hall.

FRANKLEY a small parish of 1934 acres, nearly all of it farmland, and including ancient Bromwich Wood and Frankley Beeches, 829 feet above sea level, from which 7 counties can be seen.

FRANKLEY BEECHES

EGG HILL FARM

EGGHILL DINGLE

the rise in numbers of the mighty Shire Horse as it became a useful and established breed. Both Ray and his father, at Egg Hill Farm, saw the breed at its very best during the first third of the twentieth century. The placid strength of these huge horses, many of which weighed about a ton, was in great demand for hauling heavy loads in both town and country, and they were also exported abroad. But at the end of the Second World War Ray saw the abrupt disappearance of all the heavy horse breeds from Great Britain. As tractors came in so the horses were slaughtered and they very nearly became extinct.

As he was the eldest son, Ray's childhood was hard. He was no great scholar but he liked mechanical devices. When he left Frankley school he wanted to work at the new Longbridge motor works but this idea was given short shrift by his father. The destiny of a farmer's son was farm work and Ray must work on the farm. That was final. So he began what he was later to recall as fifteen years of slave labour.

"Dad was a gentleman, and honest," he said. "He was quite forward thinking, you know. He was one of the first round our way to buy a binder, a Massey Harris it was. But he was a slave driver, and, by God, he didn't half have a temper when roused!"

From when he left school, and even before that, Ray was expected to work on the farm like a man. He tackled all the jobs on the farm, learning to do everything from hedging and ditching and muck spreading to milking cows and breaking horses. Although his father kept pigs Ray did not have much interest in them, in fact he disliked them, and the younger brothers, when they were old enough, took care of these. Sheep were not kept at Egg Hill and so Ray never learned very much about them. Always his main interest was horses and these he loved.

He recalled a traumatic day of his youth: "It was in the Great War, when I was about fifteen. Dad had promised a load of hay to Davenport Breweries in Bath Row in Birmingham and with him a promise was a promise, but there was only me to take it, and we were short of horses. All the best had been shipped to France. The government had taken horses from everywhere. There was some as tried to hide their best horses in a barn somewhere, but they were found out in the end. Anyhow I set off with the load and the three horses as we had got to pull it, but one was a mare in foal and near to foaling. It was about ten miles there and ten miles back. It was a lot for a lad of my age, y'know.

"Anyroad, we got there all right. The hay was for the brewery horses. I had to take back a load of brewery waste as Dad could use for fertiliser and it was a heavy load. I had the mare in the lead so as she had a lighter load than the other two and we got goin'. We were still some miles from home when the mare lay down in her traces in the middle of the road. I was in a fair panic, I can tell you. I managed to get her unhitched and the foal was born onto the grit of the road. I didn't know what to do.

"As it happened there was a gang of soldiers working in a field nearby and they came over and saw the trouble I was in. They helped me calm the other two horses and when the foal could stand we got it with the mare into the field.

"Well, I still had to get home with the load but now I only had two horses to pull it and there were several hills to get up on the way. I thought of unloading some of the waste but I didn't do it for fear of what Dad would say, coming home with half a load. I had to work out a way back that avoided the worst hills. It was a terrible day. When I got home it was near eleven o'clock at night. I was worn out. Dad never even give me a word of praise, y'know.

"The mare and foal had to be left in that field where they were until the foal was strong enough to make the walk home, but it thrived well. The soldiers made a proper pet of it and it used to frisk about in the field and take tit-bits from them."

At that time it was fashionable for Shires to have an abundance of hair on their legs. This made them more prone to suffer from "grease" than breeds with less hair and their legs would become inflamed and itchy. If touched on their legs the horses would kick out. "We had a mare called Violet that we bred ourselves at Egg Hill. She got 'grease' once, but she had to go to the blacksmith's at Northfield. When he lifted her hoof she kicked and twitched so much and kept backing away 'til her backside was hard up against the wall. But that didn't stop her. She backed up a bit more and backed right out, taking down part of the wall and a window. As it happened the smith was delighted. He took advantage of the demolition work to have a double door put in. He'd been thinking about it for a long time."

While his father was a stern taskmaster to his sons, neither did his mother tolerate any shilly-shallying. She was not a soft and affectionate mother but rather a practical and efficient one. Because she was his mother, Ray did love her, but he thought her hard. Yet with seven boys to look after, the dairy, the poultry and the general running of the farmhouse to see to, she had little time to give in caring for individual members of the family. In some ways it was "everyone for himself". She was proud of her dairy and she was a good cook. She had a bread oven for loaves and pies, while other cooking was done in the ovens on either side of the big black-leaded grate or on the fire itself. There was a water pump outside the back door and two pumps as well in the kitchen: one served a water butt for soft water.

At threshing time water could be a problem. Ray remembered: "The threshing machine travelled with the steam engine. The driver of the engine and the man who fed the drum on the thresher always had their food free in the house, but the others all brought their own food. One man carried water all day to supply the engine and it took a hell of a lot. The water had to come from the well, of course; it had to be continually pumped and carried in buckets. Another man carried the sacks of corn away and another the "rowins" (the chaff and husk) which was collected on a big sheet and pulled away to a heap. Sometimes we sold the rye straw to Marsh and Baxter's for wrapping hams in. During the war some straw was tied with wires into bales and sent to France."

Often at harvest the corn ricks were built on the ground on a raft of tree branches, but sometimes the old staddle stones were still used to support the rick and make it more difficult for rats to get into the straw and the grain. Ray recalled: "I'll never forget once when we were building a rick on staddle stones. Uncle Walter was up on the rick and it was built up pretty high. The

SCYTHE used for cutting hay and corn

Corn Cockle

Corn Marigold

For sharpening the scythe:

Strickle, made of oak and smeared in grease and sand.

Rubber, made of sandstone

Blade, different lengths of blade for different crops.

moveable Nibs, doles or tacks, which are adjusted to a distance equal to elbow from knuckles.

Snaith, sneth or batt.

Grass nail

Tang

Young beginners should make a habit of drawing the left hand sharply round and near to the left leg at the end of the stroke.

The cutting stroke should be flat and not scooped, with the arms guiding the scythe, but all the strength being in the back.

stones twisted and Walter felt the rick move. As it happened the rick fell straight down between the stones and if Walter had stayed on top he would have been all right, but he jumped off it and broke a leg."

All his life Ray was rarely without an elastic bandage which he wore round his left knee. "No, I never went to the war. Oh yes, I was called up when I was seventeen, but it was my knee, you see. Once I was just standing looking into a shop window and I turned away and found myself on the ground. It was the cartilage as come out. After that it slipped out often and let me down. They didn't pass me fit because I couldn't march. That's what kept me out. Dad was glad, of course."

By 1915 labour on farms was becoming increasingly difficult to obtain as more men were called up to fight. In the First World War the government, somewhat belatedly, set up committees to advise, and indeed to coerce, farmers into producing more food for the population. It was 1917 before the Agricultural Executive Committees prevailed upon the farmers to plough up more grassland and to plant more cereal crops. In Worcestershire in 1918 there were very few tractors in the county which were available for use by the Committee, and owing to unreliability, waiting for repairs or bad weather, these were more often than not out of use. The horse provided the power to work the land.

County Executive Committees for England and Wales were given powers by the government to offer advice to farmers, instruct them to plough, assist with labour and equipment, and even to terminate the tenancy and take over the land of any man who was not cultivating his land to their satisfaction. Farmers could appeal back to their county committees if they felt that the ploughing orders were unreasonable, and indeed many did so, but they were denied the right of appeal for arbitration to an independent court. The President of the Board of Agricuture and Fisheries, who set these powers in motion was Ronald E. Prothero. Later he was to become Lord Ernle.

During the First World War the Committees were reluctant to seize land, although they did actually appropriate nearly 50,000 acres. They succeeded in persuading farmers to plough a great many more acres and so to increase the

country's food supply. In 1918, at the end of the war, their directives gradually lost impetus as more and more farmers appealed against the Committees' instructions; in addition the right to appeal for arbitration in an independent court was restored to any tenant or landowner.

Ray's younger brothers, one by one as they grew old enough, joined him in working for their father on Egg Hill Farm: George junior, Harold and Quintin. Stanley, however, was apprenticed to a butcher and Bob did have aspirations to be a chemist for a while, but eventually returned to the farm.

"Dad was ill in bed with 'flu or summat. He told Harold and me to carry on with breaking a young horse as we had then. Well, we had him in a bridle on a long rein in the field when all of a sudden he took fright. We never even saw what upset him. Anyroad he reared up and he reared so high he fell over backwards and landed with a terrible crash. The horse lay still and never moved.

'Christ, he's dead!' Harold said. 'Whatever are we going to say to Dad?'

"We were worried to death as to what we were going to tell Dad and we went off back towards the house. When we got to the rickyard we saw George. 'What can we do?' we asked him, but all he could say was 'Bloody glad it was you and not me!' We couldn't think what we were going to say. Well, while we were standing there wondering what to do we heard a thud of galloping hooves and then we saw a horse galloping across the next field.

'Hey! What hoss is that?' Harold says, really puzzled. And then it dawned on us. The hoss had risen up from the dead. He must have hit his head on a stone when he fell and been stunned. By God! Relief flooded through us, I can tell you! We never did tell Dad anything about it!"

CHAPTER TWO

The Town Wife

When the war was over farmers expected that the guaranteed prices for wheat and oats would continue. Generally they had done well for themselves during the war. Feeling secure, many tenant farmers sought to buy their farms and many landowners were willing to sell. Indeed about a quarter of the land of England changed hands by 1921, very often at a high price. Fortunately Ray's father did not buy Egg Hill. To the dismay of all, the Corn Production Act which had guaranteed the prices was repealed in 1921. Farming went into a decline and many of those who had borrowed to buy their farms were in trouble.

In 1920 the weekly wage for a farm worker had been about 46 shillings (£2.30), but by 1925 it had gone down to about 36 shillings (£1.80), and at this it stayed for a further ten years. Ray did not receive a regular weekly wage from his father. Living at home as he did, his board and lodging were free and he had few expenses, but if he needed any money for anything in particular he was obliged to ask for it. There was little money to spare, but Ray's father treated him in the same way as a great many other farmers' sons were treated. They were tied by strong bonds of duty to the family business, they went in awe of their parents and they did not expect very much more from life.

In the mid-twenties Ray somehow got together the money to buy an Irish hunter called Pat. Occasionally he would manage a day off work in the winter and go out with the Albrighton Woodland pack. As a farmer's son, and as the hounds hunted occasionally over Egg Hill Farm, he did not, of course, have any subscription to pay; he had only to equip himself with decent breeches, boots, jacket and bowler hat.

He loved the quiet waiting at covert-side, the winding of the horn that sent heart and blood racing, the pounding gallops over winter fields, the adventures at hedges, but, as he never did like to kill anything, he preferred the fox to get away and live to run again. He liked to mix with the wealthy and influential people in the field, and to touch the brim of his hat with his crop and smile at the ladies. The hunting field brought all classes of people together, where, in many ways, all became equal. A lord on a blood horse might not necessarily be as good a horseman as a farmer on a sturdy cob, nor might he know the lie of the land as well.

Every year, in the manner of country landlords with large estates, Lord Cobham held a dinner at Hagley Hall for all his tenants. Sometimes Ray attended. One year he was especially keen to go as there was to be venison on the menu and this he had never tried. "Well, when it come and I tasted it, it was awful. It was like mouldy mutton. I just couldn't eat it but I didn't like to leave it on the plate, it didn't seem right, summat special like that. I kept hoping a dog would come in as I could slip it to, but none did. Anyhow I felt under the table and found a ledge and when nobody was looking I slipped the meat onto the ledge. I've often wondered if anybody ever found it there!"

Ray eventually bought himself a motor-bike and on this he was able to travel further afield, to go to dances on Saturday evenings and meet girl friends. He took out several girls, but one Saturday evening he found himself at Tardebigge village hall, between Bromsgrove and Redditch in

Worcestershire. There he met a girl who was to share his life for over fifty years. She, too, was called Isabel, but usually he called her Bid.

Many years later Bid wrote her memoirs. She said: "Mabel and I, and her friend Beatrice, had arranged to go to a Farmer's Club dance with my fiancé, but the night before he had sent me word to say he could not come with us as it was the anniversary of his father's death and his mother would be offended."

Bid felt guilty about going to the dance without him, but she went to keep Mabel and Beatrice company and, besides, she loved to dance the Charleston. Ray and one or two of his pals joined the girls at their table. Bid said: "I just had to laugh! We'd dropped cake crumbs all over the floor where we were sitting, and this chap said: 'Better let the chickens in, hadn't we?' I collapsed into giggles.

"He was jolly, full of fun," she said, "and I imagined life with him would never be dull. We danced many times and I asked myself why did it happen that my fiancé could not be there. A strange coincidence, which changed my life."

Bid was a town girl, and the idea of chickens coming indoors was not one which she normally entertained. This country chap made her laugh, and he was so lively and good looking, she knew that whatever happened it would not be fair to stay engaged to a fiancé whom she found dull. She went back to Redditch and told the man that she could not marry him.

And so it came about that Frederick William

Albrighton Woodland Hunt covered the Frankley area, established in 1908 as a separate pack from the Albrighton. It covered about 375 square miles with the hounds being kennelled at Kinver, (12 miles from Frankley, as the crow flies, on the far side of the Clent Hills).

from an oil painting by George Raybould.

FOXHOUNDS have been carefully bred since the latter half of the 1600's to hunt with stamina and patience true to the line of scent. Hounds are counted in couples. A pack may consist of 15½ couples.

The dusky night rides down the sky
And ushers in the morn,
The hounds all join in glorious cry
The hounds all join in glorious cry
The huntsman winds his ho—or—rn,
The huntsman winds his horn.
And a hunting we will go,
A hunting we will go,
A hunting we will go-o-oh,
A hunting we will go.
Henry Fielding.

"Gone Away, Gone Away"

The fox and his wife, without any strife,
Said they never ate a better goose in all of their life,
They did very well without fork or knife,
And the little ones picked on the bones—oh!

Garibaldi Raybould married Marion Isabel Smith on 16 January 1929 at St George's Church, Redditch. None of Ray's family attended the wedding. It wasn't that they did not approve of the bride, they simply went about their own affairs and didn't bother. Bid found herself installed in the cottage in Egg Hill Lane, below the farm. She told Ray that he would have to tell his father that he must pay him a proper weekly wage now that he was married. She herself found a secretarial job locally, but within the year she had to give it up as her first baby was born at the end of November.

When Bid married she knew very little about farming. Redditch was a needle and fishing tackle manufacturing town. She had been brought up in a strictly Christian family where many Victorian ideals still held, and where even a swear word like "damn" was shocking. The little that she did know about farm life was gleaned from an occasional visit to Battens Farm on the Icknield Way, which was owned by her maternal grandfather, Thomas Yeomans, a builder, and which was run by aunts and uncles.

Sometimes Ray and Bid went up to the farmhouse for Sunday dinner. The family sat on red plush chairs on either side of the dining table with both its leaves pulled out and a white linen cloth laid over the top of the everyday green chenille table cover. George, at the head of the table, carved the joint of beef and the plates were passed round. Bid was always amazed at the speed with which Ray and his brothers bolted down the food as if they were in a dinner-eating race. Steamed treacle pudding then disappeared in express time, and immediately they were up and away, calling the dogs, slapping on their caps and going about their business again, leaving Bid and Isabella to clear up. No time was ever wasted in that house.

Ray went to work on Egg Hill Farm every day and Bid was left at the cottage with the baby. "I was lonely, being far from my old family home and having been used to many friends at work. I always found Egg Hill Farm house cold, from the keen winds blowing across the reservoirs nearby, and they were blowing, too, around the cottage garden." Bid found that Ray's family was, most of the time, too busy to pay her much attention. Her mother-in-law was brisk and bustling, always occupied, with no time for feminine chit-chat. Bid admired her for her industry and skill and felt herself to be extremely inferior when it came to the practicalities of being a farmer's wife. "She regularly bought dozens of yards of cotton material to make shirts for George and all the sons, and flannelette, too, for their nightshirts. She washed the material first in the copper to shrink it, before she cut the garments out, and she looped it up to dry, all along the line.

"Sometimes I pushed the pram up the hill to see my in-laws. Going into the farmyard I was always faced with a flock of geese coming towards me with wings fluttering, necks outstretched and all hissing at the tops of their voices. I learned to manoeuvre the pram so that it went towards their heads and kept them from my legs. Mother-in-law would give me a few words of advice on child rearing, not always heeded by me, as in her day they would not put the child out in all weathers as I did, but keep it in a cocoon in front of the kitchen fire." But Isabella did give Bid one good piece of advice: "Never learn to milk, my dear," she warned, "or you will be saddled with a job for life."

Bid was very much in love with her husband, even though he jokingly declared he would rather have had a calf than a baby. Well, she hoped he was only joking, anyway. She said "Having had no encouragement to read or to study, only to work, he knew so much about nature and the country: birds, trees and animals, and weather forecasting. It was all new to me and interesting."

While she felt inadequate when it came to being a farmer's wife compared with Isabella, she felt, too, that she didn't come up to standard with her father-in-law either. "I wasn't nervous of any of the farm animals except for the bull. One day he got himself out of the pen and came trotting down the hill to the gate of the field where some cows were grazing, next to our cottage garden. From the farmyard father-in-law could see me in the garden. He shouted, 'Open the gate, let him in!' But I dared not go out into the lane to do that. I immediately dashed into the house, pushing the pram and the sleeping baby with me. Ray's father must have thought, as he had doubtless thought before, that I was no good for a farmer's wife."

Bid discounted accomplishments which were to be very useful to the wife

of a poorly educated farmer. She was
good at keeping accounts, she had
excellent secretarial skills, was
proud of her grammar and
could compose a concise
business letter. Sometimes
she went to help in the
fields, leaving the baby in
her pram under the
hedge, along with the
other women workers'
children. One evening, at
the end of a day's potato
picking, it was her turn to
be amused at father-in-law
George. "I had to smile. His
face was a picture of
astonishment when he saw that
before the women went home they got
out their powder puffs and powdered their

Bid at Egg Hill Cottage, Frankley

faces, so they would look presentable on the way home. He was so old-fashioned!"

The year before the baby was born, Ray's youngest brother, Arthur, had died at the age of eleven from pneumonia, brought on, so everyone believed, by getting his feet wet. He had been buried in Frankley churchyard. The baby was to be christened there and Ray and Bid, with Ray's sister Issy, the godmother, pushed the pram across the fields to the church. Issy had a wreath to lay on Arthur's grave, but, tired of carrying it, she asked: "Do you mind if I lay it on the pram?" So saying, she laid it on top of the baby without more ado. Bid didn't like to object, but all the same she felt upset to see her first-born going to her christening underneath a wreath. Surely this must be an omen of bad luck. To add to her concern, a week or two later, Bid came out of

ROTATION OF CROPS on a field gave them greater vigour.

Different plants use different nutrients, and some, such as clovers restore nitrogen to the soil. Several courses of rotation were used, according to soil or region.

A Typical Rotation:
(The Norfolk System)

Year 1 Wheat, sown in autumn.
Year 2 Roots or potatoes
Year 3 Barley or Oats, spring sown
Year 4 Clover, peas or beans.

PREPARING THE LAND

"There's nothing better than muck. Except better muck."

MANURE SPREADING

PLOUGHING

About an acre could be ploughed in 8 hours

$$\begin{Bmatrix} 1 \text{ furrow long} \\ 1 \text{ furlong} \\ 220 \text{ yards} \end{Bmatrix} \times \begin{Bmatrix} 1 \text{ chain} \\ 22 \text{ yards} \end{Bmatrix} = \begin{Bmatrix} 4,840 \text{ square yards} \\ 1 \text{ ACRE} \end{Bmatrix}$$

In the West Midlands the terms used

to start horses : "gee up"
to stop horses : "woah"
to turn right : "gee back" or "heet"
to turn left : "come back"

Cultivators and Scufflers might then be used to break up the land

HARROWING reduced the soil to a fine tilth and dragged out couch grass.
The land was then ready for seeding

THE FARMER'S IDEAL YEAR:

Moderately cold winter.

Early and dry spring for sowing seeds.
Showers to make them grow.
Fine end of June and July for haymaking
Showers to swell the grain.
Dry August / September for harvest.
A fair autumn for ploughing and early sowing.

Clear moon.
Frost soon.

A mackerel sky bain't
long dry

A snow year is a rich year

A wet March makes a
sad harvest

As the day lengthens
so the cold strengthens

Fine weather if
swallows fly high

Ice in November to bear a duck,
Nothing to follow but sludge and muck

the cottage to find an owl perched on the pramhandle and contemplating the baby. She feared the worst, but the baby thrived.

By now Ray was desperate to leave his father's employ. "Dad was fair, I'll say that for him, but he was a slave driver and he couldn't stand anybody being late. 'Time is money,' he always said. He was a real stickler for time-keeping. What happened was this: I got into the yard just two minutes late and he turned and give me a dressing down in front of some hired hands. That was it as far as I was concerned. The last straw. I'd had enough. I had to get away."

There were farms aplenty for letting because farming was still in a depression, but Ray had very little money. Not only must the annual rent be found but he needed implements and animals to set himself up. In the end it was Bid's mother in Redditch who came to the rescue with a loan.

Ray obtained a reference which he could present to any prospective landlord from a neighbouring, much respected, farmer of long standing:

Frankley Lodge,
Northfield,
Birmingham.

1 October 1930

I have known Mr Raybould jun. during the whole of his life, his father having lived for many years on the adjacent farm to mine.

I have always considered him an industrious and practical farmer. He is very steady and his personal character is of the highest.

I sincerely wish him every success, as I understand he is about to start business entirely on his own account.

Thos. Quinney,
Alderman and JP for City of Birmingham.

It was to be another eighteen months before Ray found his own farm.

Around the precincts of the gay domain,
Full many a cottage peeps to mock the vain,
Where rosy sylvans doubt if love or life has pain.
from "Enville". Anthony Pasquin.

CHAPTER THREE

Starting Out

There were no farms available on the Hagley Estate and so Ray had to search further afield. Bid said: "We looked at small farms for sale, but with no definite result. If the land was good the house was unsuitable or too remote, though I was told not to expect to get a farm in the middle of a town."

At last Ray decided upon Falcon Farm at Enville in Staffordshire, which lay between Bridgnorth and Stourbridge. The farm was one hundred acres and the rent about £100 per annum. Relations between Ray and his father were strained for some time after Ray informed him of his intention to move to Enville, and they had little to do with each other. By the time Ray moved to his farm all communication between them had ceased and they had not spoken to one another for some time.

Ray had already bought a couple of horses so that he could start work immediately. Bounce was bought at a sale in Droitwich for 45 guineas. She had won a prize for the best mare at the sale on that particular day, while

24

Yew

Field Maple

FALCON FARM
Enville, Staffordshire

Oak

Beech

To ENVILLE
AND BRIDGNORTH

The
Hall

Home
Farm

Wall Piece

Farm
Buildings
and Cottage

Oak Tree
Piece

Lower Oak
Tree Piece

Old Oak

Ice
House

Quarry
Cottage

Mars Bank

Black Hill

Lwr. Black
Hill

Quarry
Piece

Quarry Bank

Upper Falcon
Meadow

Lwr Falcon
Meadow

Sweet
Meadow

Irishman's
Piece

Sampson's
Cave

Farmhouse

TO KINVER
AND STOURBRIDGE

FALCON FARM FIELDS

The farm buildings and
cottage at the top of the
hill (UPPER FALCON) were
built before 1688.

Elm

elderly Blackbird had been bought at Bordesley Hall, near Redditch. Ray needed a third horse and went to an auction where he began bidding for a horse he liked the look of. His father was there too, bidding for the very same horse. But when he realised he was competing against his son he stopped and afterwards went round to speak to him. After that they were again on speaking terms. Ray's third horse was not bought that day but came later, from a farm sale. Prince cost only 30 guineas because he had a slightly broken wind.

Falcon Farm house was in a valley while the main farm buildings, with an adjoining cottage, were out of sight, up the hill towards Enville. Thus Bid was at some disadvantage as she couldn't keep track of Ray's comings and goings as most farmer's wives could, and she never knew when to put the dinner on. Down at the house there was a barn, a shed for the poultry and a couple of pigsties, but the main work of the farm centred upon the buildings at the top of the hill.

When Bid entered the farmhouse for the first time on Lady Day 1932 there was a welcome smell of lavender polish everywhere which must have been used lavishly by the previous housewife. Apart from her two-year-old daughter, she was alone, left by herself to push and pull the furniture into place and to wrestle with the ancient Aga cooker that was part of the kitchen fittings. Ray had gone up to the fields even before the furniture van had departed, to plough with Bounce and Blackbird, so eager was he to begin work on his own land.

Despite three steps up from the kitchen and a walk along a passageway to the living room, as well as dangerous steep steps into a cellar that was partly hewn out of red sandstone, Bid came to love both the house and Enville. There was water laid on to the kitchen but there was neither gas nor electricity. Lighting was by oil lamps and candles. When she was an old woman she wrote: "This home was for me an earthly paradise, with its warm relaxed climate, the not-so-far-away neighbours and the friends we made through church and business."

I myself, her two-year-old daughter, cannot remember anything of those first days at Falcon Farm. Little by little my awareness grew, from the flowers in the garden to the tall laburnum tree whose golden blossoms tapped against my bedroom window, from the hens perching in the lilac bushes to the dark tunnel of box hedge under which one had to pass to reach the privy. Old Miss Thomas, the aunt of the previous tenant, lived in a cottage partitioned off from the main house and she used the privy too but she did not mind the dark bushes. "The cobwebs catch at you like ghosts," Bid cried. "How do I know there isn't a murderer waiting to get me in the lavatory when I push open the door?"

On gloomy days especially, the arching box trees created a dark and creepy tunnel. Poor Miss Thomas wrung her hands in despair as Ray chopped down the bushes. "Oh! But we shall have no privacy!" she cried. "Anyone can see us going down there now. There'll be no privacy for us ladies!" Who was likely to see her going along the path behind the barn, box hedge tunnel or not, was a puzzle, and who would care anyway? No doubt, as a Victorian girl of the 1870s she had been brought up delicately. Ray laughed in a heartless way, cut the tunnel down to stumps and a million spiders scuttled for new homes.

Miss Thomas would take my hand and we would go searching for sticks for her fire. She was like a dry twig herself, little and thin, in her straight brown coat that fluttered through the bracken. She showed me the spots inside foxglove bells, how dandelion sap would stain the fingers, and we picked harebells and lacy woodruff that had a heady scent. Home she would go with her sticks to feed crumbs to the rats and mice who kept her company during her lonely evenings. Once she said to Bid, "Have you ever noticed how every time a chicken drinks it raises its head to thank God for each sip?"

One evening Ray, Bid and I stood between the staddle stones watching an ambulance drive away up the hill. Poor Miss Thomas, dressed in her brown coat and broad-brimmed Sunday hat, had shaken hands with Ray and Bid, lightly touched the top of my head and stepped in her high button boots into the ambulance van. It bore her away to Kidderminster hospital. As the ambulance disappeared over the hill Bid sighed. "We'd better get the chickens in," she said. We stared up at their pale shapes, roosting in the lilac tree. "Silly birds, you'd think they'd know by now that they've got to go in."

"Can't leave 'em. Fox'll have the lot!" Ray waved his arms threateningly at the tree. The fowls squawked and fluttered, some flapped amongst the branches, feathers and lilac leaves wafted on the still evening. Bid produced a broom, poked a few off their perches, shooed them across the yard to their pen at the end of the barn. Ray chased a white Leghorn; feathers flew, and squawks rent the dusky quietness.

A white owl swooped, like a pale angel, from the darkness of the beech wood, to disappear against the brightening stars. Miss Thomas's cottage was dark; no familiar lamplight shone from the downstairs window, no candle-light flickered from upstairs. "We shan't be seeing her again, I reckon," Ray said shortly, as we left the hens, securely penned at last. "And she knew it, poor Miss Thomas," Bid added.

Bid carried the candle ahead of me up to bed, or "up to roost" as Ray always said, past the cellar door which was always kept closed against steep steps which descended to an arcaded cellar partly hewn out of red sandstone. The candle-light showed our ghostly reflections in the hall-stand mirror, submerged like dead faces in a black forest of hats and coats, and then it struck with a sharp yellow light in the sideboard mirror as it flared in a draught as we passed through the front room.

I lay in my large bed and contemplated the night-light flame fluttering from its saucer of water. Tomorrow morning the laburnum flowers would swing and tap against my window,

Barn Owl often makes its home near farm buildings where there are plenty of mice.

"'Tis the farmer's care that makes the field bear"

PLOUGHING

in December, January and February

The ploughman sets up a marker as an aiming point for the first furrow and he feels mortified if the furrow is not absolutely straight, as all the furrows parallel to the first will be crooked too. At the headland he turns by pressing his weight on the plough handles to lever up the share, and the horses side-step round.

FURLONG (furrow long) = 220 yds.: The longest distance a man and team can be expected to plough in a straight line.

About an acre could be ploughed in one day. The furrow is about 9 inches wide: so the ploughman walks ten or eleven miles.

changing to make kaleidoscope patterns with the clouds. Like the laburnum patterns, full of complexity and interest, so would tomorrow be for me.

Yet soon there would be no tomorrow for Miss Thomas. Ray and Bid were right. She never did come back. For ages I could not go into the wood opposite, where the woodruff, foxgloves and harebells grew and from where we had collected her sticks, without thinking of her. Soon the cottage was let to another family.

When I could walk a fair distance Bid sent me off to the fields with Ray if he was ploughing or harrowing. I would trudge behind him in the furrow trying to place my feet precisely where he had placed his. I knew his back view intimately: the greasy old cap and the rim of hair sprouting below it, raggy coat worn out at the elbows, and his wiry arms and shoulders inside it pulling this way and that as he kept the plough straight. He always wore a collar and tie when working and never went with an open neck, no matter how hot the weather.

I watched as he took a spanner and adjusted the coulter, saw the muscles on the horses' quarters bunch as they set off again; I smelled the newly turned earth shining on the ridges and studied the gleaming pebbles. I grew tired. "Unhook, Daddy!" I would cry. "Isn't it time yet to unhook?"

"Not yet. It's too early." I wandered about the field. I explored the tiny worlds of paths made by ants, small landcapes of grasses, juxtapositions of stones, soil and weeds.

"Just to the top and I'll unhook." The horses pricked their ears. Ray hauled the plough round on the headland and set it ready for the last furrow, with the horses sidestepping neatly. Away we'd go, with flights of starlings screeching overhead and the earth singing from the ploughshare. The horses were unhitched and I was swung up onto Bounce's back for a ride back to the buildings.

Sometimes I danced on my stage, which was the entrance into the yard between two old staddle stones. Once the Albrighton Woodland hounds surged along the lane like a tide and engulfed me in a flood of vigorous muscle, their shining eyes all at a level with my own, their tongues licking me, sweet hound-breath mixed with mine. The master cracked his whip from his big bay hunter and the pack flowed away, leaving me isolated upon the shore of the drive.

Bid began in earnest to be a farmer's wife but she was frequently obliged to resort to her recipe for soothing the nerves. This was a concoction of sherry whisked up with a raw egg.

If Ray had left the farm for a few hours it was inevitable that the cows would get out. Someone would pass by: "Hey, Missus, yer cows is out and heading for the village." Bid would grab her coat and rush breathlessly up the hill with me trailing behind. The heifers, knowing very well that they had broken the rules, larked about and acted more stupidly than usual, pretending that they hadn't the faintest idea in which direction she wanted them to go. If one stared at her Bid tended to back away. It would be a good hour before they were returned to the field and another half hour before the hole they had escaped through was discovered.

When Ray arrived home he would be met with: "I've begged you to make those fences safe! They seem to know you're away. I've asked you before, I've asked you a thousand times . . . I just hope you'll do something about it."

She was loath to cross a field where bullocks were grazing and she slunk along the hedgerow hoping not to attract their attention. Inevitably they saw her and they would begin to fool about, kicking up their heels and finally charging towards her, tails high, fun in their minds. "Face up to 'em. Wave your arms about," Ray advised. "They'll swerve, you see if they don't." But Bid dare not wait to see if they swerved or not. She rushed for the gate and safety.

Ray and Bid started selling milk to neighbours and built up a small round. It was Bid's task to set up the cooler, an affair of corrugated metal, and the separator. The milk, warm from the cow, would tend to curdle if not properly cooled. The separator had many shiny metal cones with holes in them and separated the cream from the milk, but the complicated machine took ages to rinse and dry afterwards.

Bid tended the ducks and fowls, but she was nervous of cockerels. While

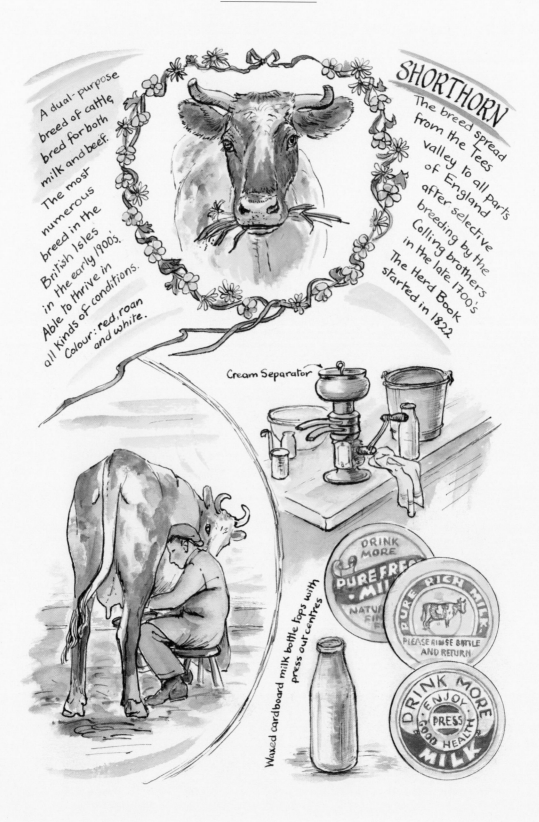

A dual-purpose breed of cattle, bred for both milk and beef. The most numerous breed in the British Isles in the early 1900's. Able to thrive in all kinds of conditions. Colour: red, roan and white.

SHORTHORN

The breed spread from the Tees valley to all parts of England after selective breeding by the Colling brothers in the late 1700's. The Herd Book started in 1822.

Cream Separator

Waxed cardboard milk bottle tops with press out centres

DRINK MORE PURE FRESH MILK NATURALLY FINE

PURE RICH MILK PLEASE RINSE BOTTLE AND RETURN

DRINK MORE MILK ENJOY PRESS GOOD HEALTH

A calf bought from market to rear, either to keep or to sell on again.

The period of gestation is about 283 days. The first milk after the calf is born is "byestings" or colostrum, which is rich, salty and high in protein. With sugar it can be made into a pudding.

A HEIFER (young female) becomes a COW after she has born a calf. She usually has her first calf at 2 to 2½ years old.

A cow's horns develop a ring every year. During the years that she bears a calf the rings are deeper. She can live to about 20 years of age.

The calf was weaned from the cow at 2-3 months old.

a non-spill milk bucket

The friendly cow, all red and white
I love with all my heart:
She gives me cream with all her might,
To eat with apple tart.   R. L. Stevenson.

Dairy Shorthorn Bull

Ray loved the sleek lines and arrogance of Indian Game birds, Bid wouldn't go to hang the washing out if the Indian Game cock were strutting under the clothes line. Sometimes if a little chick were ailing and looked as if it were about to die it was brought into the house, wrapped in an old cloth, and placed in a shoebox by the fire. Holding its head in smoke for a while was supposed to revive it.

Bid wrote, "Among our milk customers we found we could sell chickens if they were ready dressed for the oven, but I didn't know how to set about doing such a job, which is an essential sideline for a farmer's wife. In feathering the bird not much skill was required, just patience and concentration. An old country woman, who had been in domestic service at Enville Hall offered to teach me to dress them as she had done. I went across the fields to her cottage (Quarry Cottage, near the Icehouse), carrying the feathered bird on many afternoons till I knew the expert's method of dressing it, and with a sprig of parsley it looked quite professional. Then Ray would carry it away and add four or five shillings to that week's milk and cream bill."

Bid was proud of her new-found skill. "It's an art," she would say, standing back to admire her handiwork. She plucked expertly as well, hardly ever tearing the skin. When she had finished her hair was full of tiny down feathers. They clung everywhere and wafted off the newspapers that were spread about her feet to catch them.

Then she stood up and lit a twist of newspaper with a match. The paper flared and she brandished it about the plucked chicken to burn off any tiny wisps of down that remained on its skin. There was a strong smell of singeing feather and flesh. Charred bits of black paper fluttered about and settled with the feathers in her hair. "Ow! Ow!" she squawked, as she scorched her fingers on the burning brand. Ray had no stomach for killing the fowls. After one disastrous afternoon when he ended up with a sick headache, Bid's birds had to be killed by a farm hand or someone from the village.

"Why can't we have pheasants?" I wanted to know. "A cock pheasant!" I didn't care so much about the dinner he would make but more for his brilliant

A brace of pheasants with a partridge.

feathers. When the shooting season started a keeper would appear on the kitchen doorstep bearing the gift of a brace, a legitimate pair that we could eat with a clear conscience. It was surprising, though that several came to grief just outside our house, accidentally run over by the bus, perhaps! After we had eaten one killed in this way I was warned not to tell my friends at school what we had had for dinner on Sunday, or the gamekeeper would be sure to hear about it, nor was I allowed to keep the pretty feathers in case there was a spy about who would tell the gamekeeper.

In July 1934 Ray and Bid's only son Kenneth was born, and he was christened at Enville church. Bid wrote: "Ray worked very hard, all hours, as he had always done for his father, but now we had something to work for, for ourselves. I enjoyed the outdoor work in Enville's pleasant climate, rearing chickens, haymaking, and planting and picking potatoes, with Mrs Shepherd, Hilda and several young women from the village. They were jolly days. One autumn there were at least five prams under the hedge when we were potato picking. The year our son was born, five babies, all boys, were born in the vicinity. The company, the exercise, and the invigorating air were good for mothers and sons."

Soon there was another addition at the farm. She waited, uncertain and anxious to please, tied to the barn door with a length of binder twine: Nellie, a young farm collie, mostly white but with some black markings. She was sweet-natured and faithful, and was with us through all the years, right until the end at "Heartbreak Farm".

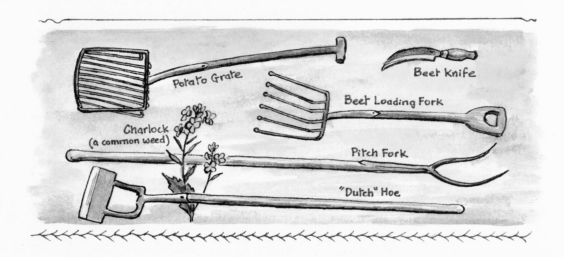

Potato Grate

Beet Knife

Charlock
(a common weed)

Beet Loading Fork

Pitch Fork

"Dutch" Hoe

CHAPTER FOUR

Work and Workers

Like most farmers Ray relied on casual labour at busy times of the year, but he did employ a lad who lived in and ate his meals with us. Dick came from a children's home, was a pleasant boy and worked well, but unfortunately he stole two gold sovereigns from Bid's dressing table, as well as some other items. Ray had to dismiss him.

The next boy was surly and brusque. Bid said she couldn't take to him but Ray said he must be given time and he would improve. One morning the boy was cleaning out the stables when Ray paused at the door to run a fond eye over the rumps of his horses as they stood in their stalls. Everything appeared to be normal but then he noticed a spot of red, shining like a berry, on Blackbird's hindquarters. On closer inspection it proved to be a drop of blood. Ray frowned over it, sticky upon his finger. It wasn't the time of year for horse flies. What could have caused it?

"I'll be blowed!" He muttered. "There's another one! And another!"

There were five bright blood spots on the black rump, five droplets, equally spaced and in a row. The boy was disappearing sullenly out into the farmyard, pushing the barrow of manure. The fork he had used was propped against the wall. One, two, three, four, five! Five prongs! Ray was furious.

"The bugger wouldn't move over," the boy said. "He just leaned on me and wouldn't budge." "Clear off," Ray shouted. "You're sacked." The children's home asked if Dick could be given a second chance, so back he came. This time he stole cigarettes from the cottage adjoining the farm buildings up on the hill and so he was again asked to leave.

"Old Bristol", whose real name was George Gilbert, was an itinerant visitor who had now added Falcon Farm to his list. For years he had helped at Egg Hill where he was not always welcome. Ray said, "Well, he'd come and work well for a while, but then, just when the work was at its peak, he'd vanish on a boozing spree and leave us in the lurch. Then someone'd notice in the paper that he'd been had up and fined a shilling for being drunk and disorderly in Stourport or somewhere. Then when we'd forgotten all about him he'd come shambling up the lane again. 'So you've turned up, you old bugger!' Dad would shout. 'Well, you can bloody well clear off again. I've washed my hands of you, this time. Clear off!' Then the old man would disappear round a bend in the lane and wait until Dad had gone out to the fields and then he'd come back and cut some sticks for Mother and ingratiate himself again. 'Oh! Do find him a job, won't you,' Mother would say. 'He'll stick to it this time,

~ "Old Bristol" ~

I'm sure he will.' But after six weeks he'd be gone again and Dad would say 'Fancy him just clearing off and leaving all that hoeing!'"

One day at Enville Ray came in laughing. "Old Bristol's coming down the lane three sheets in the wind, and his shirt tail's flapping out the back of his trousers. And Chamberlain, he pedals past on his sit-up-and-beg, and Chamberlain says, 'Hey there, my man, you've got your apron on back to front!'" Ray, convulsed with laughter, wiped the tears from his eyes. Always soft-hearted, off he went to settle Old Bristol in the barn and tell him that when he was sobered up he could set to hoeing the mangels, or, if wet, clean the horses' tack.

One morning the old man wasn't shambling about as usual. There was no billy can brewing tea, he wasn't there spitting up baccy-stained phlegm or getting a rough shave with his blunt cut-throat razor. Ray found him groaning at the bottom of the granary steps. "I've broke me back," he croaked with beery breath. At Kidderminster hospital they found he had broken his hip and it would be a long time before he was tramping again, let alone working and boozing.

Despite his pain he had managed to whisper to Ray that his pension book was hidden under a loose board in the granary floor. Ray found it there under Old Bristol's other precious possessions: his billy can, stove, and sugar and tea tins and empty beer bottles. For months Ray regularly took the pension book into Kinver post office and illegally collected the old man's pension, which he put away for when he should see Old Bristol again. Sure enough, the old man did come hobbling up the lane on two sticks one day to claim his money and all the worldly goods he had left behind in the granary.

The Merediths, too, were itinerant visitors. Mr Meredith was broad and stocky, in a ragged old coat and trousers tied below the knee with binder twine. Except when he was drunk he didn't have much to say for himself. She was tall and thin and wore a black felt hat and a long coat that flapped round her ankles. Bid was slightly shocked when she discovered they weren't actually married, but her tolerance had broadened somewhat since the days before she had met Ray.

They often came to cut swedes and mangels. Sometimes I went to the fields when they were there, making my way across the cold ground between the cheerless rows of roots. They appeared to be a companionable-looking group but

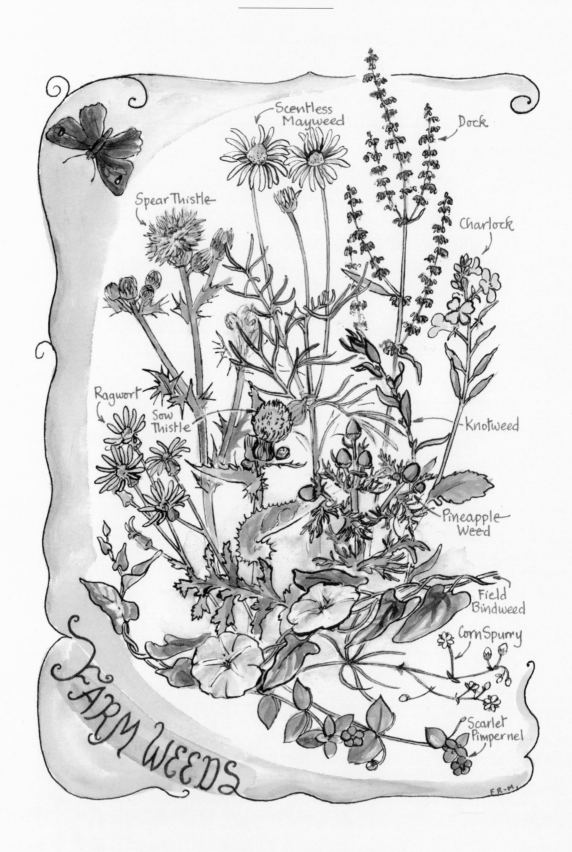

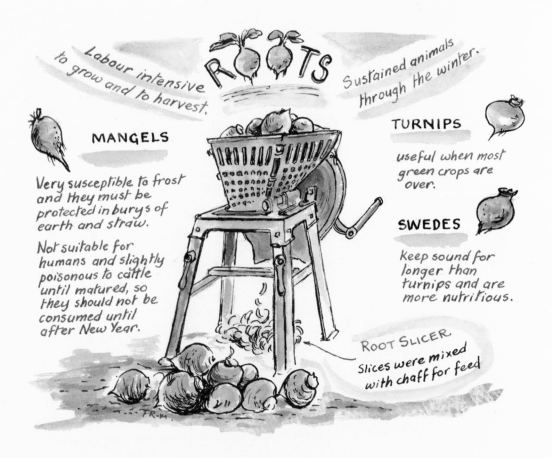

ROOTS

Labour intensive to grow and to harvest.

Sustained animals through the winter.

MANGELS

Very susceptible to frost and they must be protected in burys of earth and straw.

Not suitable for humans and slightly poisonous to cattle until matured, so they should not be consumed until after New Year.

TURNIPS

useful when most green crops are over.

SWEDES

Keep sound for longer than turnips and are more nutritious.

ROOT SLICER
Slices were mixed with chaff for feed

when I actually reached them I found that there were few words exchanged, especially when the gaffer (Ray) was there too. I would stand for a while watching their hands, reddened by the cold morning and the icy touch of the swedes. The action of the sharp knife was economically beautiful as it chopped off the clinging soil, through the purple skin and into the cream interior. There was not much entertainment in root cutting in a bitterly cold field, although I did enjoy an ice-cold sliver of crisp white swede. "You'll get a pain under your pinafore if you eat much of that," Ray would say. Mrs Meredith's thin face smiled wanly as her knife, held in red-raw hands, snick-snacked at the roots and tops.

Swedes were winter feed for the animals. Sometimes they were left growing in the field and the cattle were turned out to eat them where they grew. Mangels, too, were grown for the animals but they had to be piled into earth burys to protect them from frost until they had matured. They were eaten early in the new year.

The Merediths travelled the roads pushing an old pram which contained all their belongings. When they worked at Falcon Farm they lived in a lean-to shed, against the back of the stables. One side of it was open, but they hung a tarpaulin across the gap. They slept on straw and cooked on a wood fire outside, eating anything edible that they could lay their hands on. They knew no comforts or luxuries, except for beer.

Once, when Bid was picking potatoes alongside Mrs Meredith, Bid remarked, "Well, I haven't picked many, but I'll have to go home now and do some housework." "That's nice," said Mrs Meredith. "What I've always wanted is a house." Bid went home counting her blessings.

One cold winter they almost burned down the farm buildings. "I'd have give 'em credit for a bit more sense," Ray fumed. "They had too much to drink, I'll be bound. They've had a fire in the shed and it's a miracle the whole lot didn't go up." "The weather's been very cold," Bid said. "I do feel sorry for Mrs Meredith."

One year Ray grew a fine crop of peas. "I've sold the field," Ray told Bid. "Chap from over Brierley Hill way has bought 'em as they stand. That'll save me having to pick 'em." A gang of women arrived on the back of a lorry the following morning. They waded in, laughing and joking amongst the peas, systematically denuding the plants of every shining pod and throwing the spent plants down. They came on the following day, too, but at mid-day, when almost half the field had been picked, they began to discuss the wages that were coming to them.

"How much is he payin' you, then?" Ray asked.

"A shillin' a pot. We wants threepence a pot more, it ain't worth our while else." They decided to strike and sat on the roadside verge waiting for the lorry to come and pick them up.

That year there was a glut of peas on the market. The women did not return to finish picking the crop and neither did the man from Brierley Hill. We had some of them for dinner occasionally, the pheasants and partridges had some, and Ray organised a handful of women from the village to pick the remainder, which he used for seed the following year.

It was schooltime for me. I walked the two miles to Enville School with an older girl who had to pass Falcon Farm on her way there. A year or so later I went on a little bicycle. Many of the children at school were the sons and daughters of the tenants or estate workers of Sir John Grey. My best friend, Jean MacKenzie, was the head groom's daughter. Everyone was aware of the importance of the others in the running of the estate, and knew where each fitted in.

In September 1936 Ray and Bid's third child Christine was born and she was christened at Enville Church.

Ray bought me a pony. Her name was Dolly, she was dark brown, almost black, and she was bought from a neighbouring big house along the lane. Dolly was really a little too spirited for a first pony and I could never manage her without someone at her head. Once she took off at a gallop right across the field and I couldn't hold her. She stopped of her own accord, though, with me still on her back, feeling very inadequate. On one or two occasions Ray gave up a day's work and took me on a leading rein out with the Albrighton Woodland. He walked miles and miles on those days, all over the Sheep Walks and way beyond Enville. We saw the hounds, we saw everyone on their horses, we saw fresh fields and woods, but we never did see the fox.

My brother Ken had whooping cough and he had been very ill. Bid was worried, not only for him but for the baby, Christine, too. It was a dangerous illness. One day she came downstairs smiling. "He's not feverish any more, just talking in his sleep," she said. "He turned over and said 'Unhook, Daddy'."

My days of following the plough were over now, and it was Ken's turn. I thought nostalgically of those long mornings following in the furrow but now, when I was not at school, I wanted to try more ambitious occupations.

"Couldn't I have a go, please Dad? Could I milk old Daisy?" "You'll get kicked. I haven't got time to mess about. Let me get the job done and get off wum." His hands closed over the cow's rubbery teats and the warm milk sang

When forth I go upon my way, a
thousand toys are mine.
The clusters of dark violets, the
wreaths of the wild vine;
My jewels are primroses so pale,
the bindweed and the rose;
And show me any courtly gem
more beautiful than those. ANON.

NELL

Ken   A Visitor called Monty   Me

RABBITS

Rabbits were introduced into England by the
Normans soon after the Conquest. They were farmed
in Warrens for meat. The fur was used for such
things as clothing, felt and manure.
By the late 1700s the keeping of rabbits became unprofitable,
Warrens and rabbits were destroyed, but some animals survived.
By 1900 rabbits had become a pest.

RABBITS ATE
MILLIONS OF POUNDS—
WORTH OF CROPS. Their numbers
could not be kept under control by any known method and farmers
were at their wits end as to how to save their crops ————

CHAFF CUTTER
driven by a motor
or turned by hand.

Hay pushed in here

Water to dampen chaff mixed with other ingredients.

cutting blade

cut edge of hay

chaff
(hay, sometimes oat straw, chopped into half inch lengths)

into the pail in two continuous streams. How easy it looked! Eventually I tried and what an effort it was to extract a drop, let alone to make a froth in the pail.

Bid took us to see the steam rollers that were repairing the lane, and, more particularly, to smell the tar that the workmen were pouring onto the road. The hot tar scent was supposed to be good for coughs.

When he was better again Ken and I trailed Ray around the farm, riding up on the horses, and up on the loads. I loved to be in the barn when he was mixing the feed for the horses: a shovel full of chaff, then some bran, a few oats, a splash of water, and then the scrape, scrape of the shovel on the concrete floor as it was all mixed together. There was a row of bins in the barn containing animal foodstuffs. I sampled them all: the dry bran, linseed cattle cake, and flaked maize, which was my favourite. I even chewed hay in an effort to discover why the animals liked it so much. Then what satisfaction it was to stand in the stable on a gloomy evening after work was done and listen to the horses munching their bait. It was one of the very happiest sounds I could imagine.

In the stable Ray kept a sack with a slit in its side hanging on the wall. Into this he pushed all the combings from the horses' manes and tails. Now and then a rag and bone man or a gypsy would call and pay a shilling for a full bag. If tail hair had been kept separate from mane hair, then the tail hair would fetch more than a shilling. The combings from a grey horse were worth twice as much. Eventually the hair would be used for stuffing furniture or making brushes.

I tried to swing a scythe and to cut swedes with the robot style that only comes from long practice. I studied the field pebbles, always searching for the non-existent flawless white one, I inspected the weeds, the caterpillars and mouseholes. I visited Mrs Haines at her cottage by the boundary wall where she showed me the first patchwork quilt that I had ever seen and which I considered was quite wonderful. I admired the velvety mulleins that grew on the walls near her house.

Sometimes we had visitors or campers in the fields. One hot summer day someone's daughter came with a swimming costume and we went to the pond. She ventured to the edge of the water. Her pale toes stirred up a fine silt on the bottom as she turned, beckoning me to follow her. I declined. I had seen the cows standing in there. I had seen all manner of creepy crawlies in the water and gnats hovering over it in eddying clouds in the evenings. No. I didn't want to paddle either. Honestly! In a duck pond!

The pond was sepia, reflecting tawny clouds, with lily leaves and dragonflies skimming the surface nearer to the centre of it. A small group of us watched as she waded in, the mud oozing between her toes in tobacco brown eddies that finally clouded the water into an unattractive muddy mess. Undeterred, she plunged into clearer, as yet unsullied water and floundered for a stroke or two.

After a couple of minutes she rose up gasping. "Ow! Uuh! Look! Uuh! Look!" Her eyes were wide with horror. Tadpoles slithered all over her. She pinched the costume away from her skin and peered down her chest and they were wriggling all over her body.

"I'll fetch some water." Bid ran for the house, snatched up a milk pail and filled it from the tap, meanwhile we slopped pond water over the poor girl and managed to swill a few tadpoles off her.

Bid tipped the pail of ice-cold water over her head and she screeched with the shock of it but it flushed the remainder of the tadpoles off her. I noted that many of them were growing their legs and worried that they wouldn't all find their way back into the pond.

Ken and I made dens in the bracken in the beech wood, sometimes we saw a kingfisher at the pond and we opened an ant hill and saw tiny white ant eggs. We got in the way of Ray's work. "I've got a job to do," he would impatiently declare. "I can't be bothered with that now. Just let me get the job done. And keep your fingers away from that chaff-cutter."

In later years Ray said: "Sometimes when I was at Enville I had bad dreams about how I was behind-hand with the work." He was usually in a hurry. At tea time he would gulp down pickled damsons and thick buttered bread, then a large slice of cake, meanwhile impatiently stirring three spoonfuls of sugar into his tea. Round and round whipped the spoon in the cup which grated on Bid's nerves. "It's no good talking, Bid," he would say.

"Well, can't you wait a bit then?"

"I've got work to do!" He poured the tea down his throat, slammed the cup into its saucer, slapped the cap onto his head and was striding away up the hill to fetch the cows in for milking. Bid was left, complaining crossly about the heap of sugar that remained still undissolved in the bottom of the cup.

The scent of clover wafted sweetly on the breeze. Fields full of it rippled like a green sea with wave after wave of blowing perfume. Mixed with the clover there was hare's foot, ladies' fingers, centaury and hop medick, a trillion blossoms stirring under the June sun. The whirr of the mower's blades purred across the fields and sometimes the singing of stone against blade as someone honed a scythe. Ray rode the mower behind Blackbird and Bounce while Nell was miserable, whining in the barn where she had been confined in case she got in the way of the mower's sharp blades. The blades snicked back and forth, horizontally, along the ground. Every now and then the horses had a

Haytime

Fields of grass and clover are cut in June when the grasses are coming into flower. The crop is dried in the sun and wind to make HAY. This is fodder for animals during the winter months.

When cut the grass falls into swathes on the ground. It is left to dry on the top and then tedded, (shaken and turned), so that it dries out further.

If there is rain it must be tedded again. To make good hay several dry days are needed. If there is a large amount of clover the crop will take longer to dry out.

keep half the straw and half the hay For the worst of winter at Candlemas Day

Cock's Foot

Rye Grass

Meadow Grass

Meadow Foxtail

Yorkshire Fog

TWO-HORSE MOWER

the blade is dropped to horizontal position when mowing

Cost of machine in 1939 = £25-7s.6d

haycocks, to be collected in a wagon and taken for stacking.

HAYMAKING

Raking the mown grass into "rows" for drying. It was then turned again before piling into "cocks"

rest while Ray laboriously sharpened with a file each edge of the V-shaped serrations of the blades.

With a gentle breeze and a warming sun the flat rows of cut grass and clover dried and paled. The Merediths arrived to turn the hay into long fleecy rows so that it would dry thoroughly and then Prince, in the horse-rake, was brought in to turn it yet again.

"I'll be carrying tomorrow, if it keeps fine." He found extra help from somewhere: a man borrowed from another farm or perhaps a pair of campers. Bid was there carrying flasks of tea and cider. Nell was free now, on the look-out for rabbits, and there would be rides on the wagon from the rick yard to the field every time the wagon was unloaded. "These fire a stack, quick as a match," Ray said, pulling out a broad-leaved plantain from a mass of hay. At the best of times hay stacks generated heat, but if the crop had been carried when it was still very slightly damp and it included large green leaves then spontaneous combustion could easily occur.

When winter came Ray stood on top of the stack and cut it into chunks with a hay knife. Brown scorch marks sometimes became apparent. "We were lucky here," he would say. "This has hotted up. It could have fired."

Haymaking done, Ray set about writing a newspaper advertisement for a boy to help and in due course one was found. Norman Shepherd was a local boy. "He won't need to live in," Ray said. "He lives on Enville Common and can walk over every day." He was a gangling lad, with a long, but cheerful, face. His bony limbs stuck out, scarecrow-like, from his sleeves and trousers. He set to, willingly, to mow down thistles, groom horses, clean cow sheds and help with the harvest.

The green corn was yellowing fast and toasting through gold to raw sienna. The harvest was never good at Falcon Farm. The rabbits ate up the young green shoots as fast as they pushed through the earth. All along the hedgerows the rabbits had their burrows and they ate well into the fields, all the way round. Ray grew oats, which were fuel for the horses, and, unlike the straw of wheat or rye, oat straw could be used to feed the animals. He grew some wheat and rye, which he often planted on the field called Irishman's Piece, which was poor, sandy soil.

Harvest was a hard time for Norman, coming straight from school and not having had time to toughen up his muscles properly. It was hard work for anyone, even fit men. Sitting up on the binder Ray had many things to keep an eye on all at once, from the three horses who were harnessed to it, to the blades, the canvasses, the supply of twine and looking out for stones that might foul the blades.

For Norman it was a time of trying to make a stook stand up. "You do this," Ray demonstrated while giving the horses a breather. He grasped a sheaf in each hand, planted them firmly upright and leaned them so that the ears mingled and they supported one another, then he added two more to one side of the pair, two to the other side, and two at either end. If the rain came down before they were carried it should run down from the ears along the stalks and to the ground. If properly placed not even a strong wind could blow them down. Norman tried hard. Ray watched. "No, no!" Ray hopped up and down. He had little patience. "Like this." Norman tried again. Ray threw up his arms in despair and stomped back to the binder.

Ray rested the horses often and climbed down from the seat to gulp a mouthful of cold tea. He'd rub some ears of corn into the palm of his hand, blow the husks off and nibble the grains, while he surveyed Norman's work. "Try to keep 'em in lines, will yer?" He sighed. "Makes it easier to run the wagon straight through when we come to carry."

When there was only a small patch of corn left standing in the middle of the field it was usually the haven of many rabbits. As the patch grew smaller anyone round about who had a shotgun appeared to pick them off as they ran out. Sometimes they broke from the standing corn four or five at a time and the lads cheered and took aim.

Carrying the crop was the hardest work. It could never be done in a leisurely manner for there were often thunderstorms brewing as well as several more fields waiting to be cut and carried before the weather broke.

"Hold tight!" was the regular cry to the man on top of the load as the horses dug their toes into the ground, muscles bunching, snorting through cracking nostrils, sweat-sticky manes bouncing on wet necks, flies clouding the air above their heads as they surged forwards. Leather and chains creaked under the strain, wagon wheels cracked and crunched stones, and Nell ran alongside, barking encouragement. "Hold tight! Hey hup there!" Another enormous effort and the last load was on the move with the horses careering forwards. The helpers who were giving a half-hearted push at the back of the wagon nearly fell flat on their faces as the horses bounded towards the rick yard.

Ray took a pride in his rick building. "You see as how I'm sloping it out a bit as we go up," he explained to Norman who passed the sheaves up from the wagon. "That way it won't piddle itself." Norman, covered in chaff and sweat,

SHEAF of corn, sometimes called batin, boltin or shock.

A MIDLANDS BOND KNOT, as tied by Ray

The tie was executed in different ways according to different regions, the method having been passed down from old men to boys in the field over many generations.

The bond of straw was pulled by the right hand out of the bundle while the sheaf was held in the crook of the left arm, and the tie was made, all in a few seconds.

Before the days of machines the corn was cut by scythes and tied into sheaves by hand

When mechanical horse-drawn BINDERS were used the corn round the edge of the field still had to be cut with a scythe and bound by hand. The field had to be "opened up" for the Binder.

The mechanical BINDER cut the corn and tied it with binder twine into sheaves, which the machine ejected onto the ground.

cold tea

Binder Twine made from Empire grown Sisal

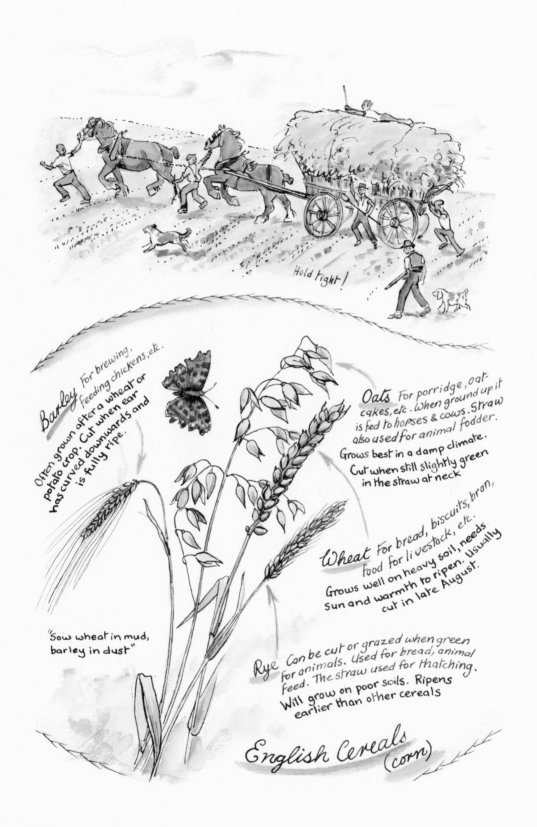

Hold tight!

Barley For brewing, feeding chickens, etc. Often grown after a wheat or potato crop. Cut when ear has curved downwards and is fully ripe.

Oats For porridge, oat-cakes, etc. When ground up it is fed to horses & cows. Straw also used for animal fodder.
Grows best in a damp climate. Cut when still slightly green in the straw at neck

Wheat For bread, biscuits, bran, food for livestock, etc. Grows well on heavy soil, needs sun and warmth to ripen. Usually cut in late August.

"Sow wheat in mud, barley in dust"

Rye Can be cut or grazed when green for animals. Used for bread, animal feed. The straw used for thatching. Will grow on poor soils. Ripens earlier than other cereals

English Cereals (corn)

opened his mouth vacantly. "I mean as the rain won't drip down the sides of the rick. It'll fall off the eaves instead." Norman nodded, passing up another sheaf. "The sides slope out so's at the top they're a foot outside the base."

The ricks were built on a three feet deep layer of hedge brushings but the weight of the straw flattened them down to a thickness of a few inches. These were sufficient to allow air to rise and to stop damp from penetrating upwards. As Ray reached the eaves he began to peer anxiously at the number of sheaves that were still to be tossed up to him. The big question was, would there be enough to complete the rick properly? It was a poor rick builder who had calculated wrongly. A good man could judge the size of the crop as it grew in the field and so have a fairly accurate idea as to the dimensions of the rick.

After the last load was carried the fowl ventured into the field to peck the remaining grain, flocks of birds descended upon it and two or three women from the estate cottages arrived to glean any stray ears they could find, not for corn to make bread as they would have done in the old days, but to feed their chickens.

The bracken in the woods turned yellow, gold and then copper, the leaves on the beech trees opposite the house crisped from gold to bronze and swallows grouped themselves along the telegraph wires in readiness for their winter journeys.

After potato picking time the threshing machine came. I needed no warning to keep my distance from it. It was a great rattling box-like contraption, almost as big as a cottage, with leather belts hurtling round pulley wheels. Whirling chaff and dust billowed from it in choking clouds. Accompanying it came a steam traction engine which powered the thresher and which pulled it along the lanes as it travelled from one job to another.

The unknown men who worked on it slaved incessantly to keep the sheaves going in and to remove the sacks of grain, the straw and the chaff. Nell slunk about, hoping for a bit of sport with a rat, but was really waiting for the moment when Ray would be forced to leave it and fetch up the cows for milking. Bid peeled mountains of potatoes towards the dinner of two of the men.

At last the monster chugged away and the farm resumed its normal life. On winter afternoons I ran across the fields to inspect Norman's hedge brushing prowess. His hands were bound in old rags to protect them from thorns. Sometimes he had a bonfire going, the flames exotic in the grey landscape, a feast for the eyes. We shoved potatoes into the embers and they came out over-cooked on one side and raw on the other. We ate them in a bitter east wind and, like the potatoes, we froze on one side and cooked ourselves against the fire on the other. When the fire was dead there were long sticks of charcoal to be rescued from the grey ash to be carried home for drawing pictures. "He's a good lad, Norman is," Ray pronounced. "He's a good worker."

Nellie had puppies. We kept one for a few months. He was my close companion. "Call him Jock," Norman advised. "He'll come if you call him Jock." How I loved that little dog! But then Ray sent him away to a new owner and how I grieved and cried and longed for him to escape and come back to me. I looked out for him for days, but he had only been a pup and would never have been able to find his way back to Falcon Farm.

It was an evening in January 1938, the 25th: "Can that be Enville Hall that's on fire?" Bid asked. It was dusk, but the red sky was no normal sunset. It shimmered and glowed in the strangest way. We stood outside the farmhouse gaping at the display of red, orange and purple light that shone above the dark woods until it faded away at last, leaving just an ordinary night sky. Next day the mystery was solved. The newspapers reported that the Northern Lights, the aurora borealis, had been visible, giving their finest display in England in this century.

Later that same month there were severe gales and trees blew down all over the estate, keeping the Enville saw-mill busy. Several elms came down near our farm buildings. In the woods large trees blew against yew trees, knocking them over fences into fields. Some of Ray's heifers ate the yew and died with it in their mouths. Ray worried about his horses. He had a fine colt called Orby for which he felt no compensation from the Hall could be adequate. Fortunately neither Orby nor any of the other horses ate the yew and the Estate hurried to remove all the fallen timber and leaves. That year the Estate

ENVILLE
STAFFORDSHIRE

Angel. ~ sketch of detail on misericord carved in the late 1400's in St. Mary's

The pink sandstone church of St. Mary's looked over the blacksmith's, the school, two or three shops, The Cat Inn, the war memorial and Stamford House, which had once been an hotel and accomodated visitors who came to visit Enville Hall's famous gardens.

POPULATION OF ENVILLE IN THE 1930'S
WAS ABOUT 650
There were about 80 children at the school, 3 teachers: Mr. Anderson, head teacher, Mrs. Jackson and Miss Shingler.

THE FINEST CRICKET GROUND IN ALL ENGLAND IN THE 1800'S

Adjacent to the Hall, the ground was believed to be superior to Lords, being perfectly level and smooth. The Rt. Hon. George Grey was president of Marylebone Cricket Club in 1851

Still a splendid ground in the 1930's.

Enville School, Erected in 1861 by the Countess of Stamford and Warrington.

The **ENVILLE ESTATE** encompassed 4980 acres and was owned by Sir John Foley Grey. The Greys first came into possession in 1528 and acquired the titles Earl of Stamford & Warrington. Enville's medi-eval manor house was replaced before the mid 1500's, and over the centuries the house was rebuilt and enlarged.

TELEGRAMS
KINVER 60

John Grey

On the edge of the Sheepwalks SHENSTONE'S CHAPEL was built. William Shenstone, 1714-1763, poet and landscape architect laid out Enville Hall's gardens. Other attract-ions, including a spectacular conservatory, were added in mid 1800's. 73 acres of gardens were maintained then by 35 men and boys. (Arthur Avery head gardener in 1930s.

Near Lyndon Covert SAMPSON'S CAVE was partly hewn into rock and partly built with sandstone by Sampson Allen in the mid 1700s, in a similar style to the caves nearby at Kinver. Sampson's Cave was still lived in in the early 1950's.

From 1903 until 1940's Mr. George Arthur Raddon Chamberlain was Agent for the Estate.

waived half of Ray's yearly rent. Later in the year Sir John himself lost twelve bullocks when a yew tree crashed across a fence into a meadow.

Enville was beautiful, with its deep woods of beech, oak and rhododendrons, its ponds and its secret places, like the Icehouse, Sampson's Cave and Shenstone's Chapel. The woods were full of pheasants, Sir John's pheasants, and the gamekeeper hung rows of dead weasels and other pheasant predators on the fences. The gamekeeper was to be feared; he could sometimes put down poison that might kill Nellie. That was the reverse of the idyll, as were the yew trees.

One day Ray came home with news: "Sir John's dead." "What'll happen now?" Bid asked. "I dunno, seeing as how he was a widower and young Eileen hasn't come of age yet. I dunno what they'll do."

Enville Hall was closed up. Most of the staff was given notice, the horses sold, the furniture swathed in dust cloths and the shutters drawn. Only a gardener was kept on, and a caretaker. My friend at school, Jean, whose father was head groom, told me one day that they were soon to leave their house. I thought I would lose my friend, but there were actually good times to come, for her father was made the caretaker and the family went to live in a suite of rooms at the Hall.

What joy it was to visit her! What excitement! We had a labyrinth of corridors, stairs, halls and silent rooms to lose ourselves in. We had about seventy acres of gardens, shrubberies, lakes and woodland with follies, fountains and arbours all to ourselves. It was magic, even the frightening places, when we went along passageways opening doors at random expecting to surprise a terrible ghost inside. Nerves taut as bowstrings, we scared ourselves silly when we came upon a chamber of death, where dozens of glazed eyes all stared hostilely as we peeped round the door, as if we had interrupted the creatures in a debate. Shrieking we raced away along the endless corridors. All the mounted masks of foxes and heads of bucks had been put in here for storage, together with stuffed birds under glass domes.

From the walkway round the roof we could see right across the Hall's landscaped grounds, the rhododendron plantations, the Sea Horse pond, where statuary sea horses curled stone fishes' tails amongst the waxy water lilies, and the rose gardens. You could see the green velvet cricket field, the grouped horse chestnut trees in the park and the Home Farm pond, where Billy and Norman Bullock fished for eels.

Those were days of sunshine and enchantment, where ghosts wafted round us with the scent of roses but always kept their distance, where all the mysteries of the Hall's dark corridors and deep woods were benign ones, and all the world was ours.

There were a couple of small shops in Enville village and two or three in the opposite direction at Potters Cross, where Ray's brother Stanley had his butcher's business. There were several shops in Kinver and most weeks a travelling shop came round, crammed with everything from tins of polish to cabbages. Sometimes we went by bus to Stourbridge for, perhaps, a new pair of desperately needed children's shoes or some knitting wool. Bid was obsessively careful with money. It was all hard won and she had very little of it. Once, in Stourbridge, Ray pointed out a railway bridge to me. "Under that bridge the Black Country begins," he said. I peered along the street and under the bridge but could see nothing strange. What kind of a country could it be through there? For years I wondered.

An occasional excursion, especially if we had a visiting aunt and uncle, would

Stable Windowsill

ELLIMANS
ROYAL
EMBROCATION
FOR HORSES

Tippers
VITALIS

Brass-covered Hames.

Yet when from plough or lumbering cart set free,
They taste awhile the sweets of liberty;
E'en sober Dobbin lifts his clumsy heel
And kicks, disdainful of the dirty wheel;
But soon, his frolic ended, yields again
To trudge the road, and wear the clinking chain.
                        Robert Bloomfield 1766–1823

Cart Harness

Plough Harness

3 HORSES WERE REQUIRED FOR A FARM OF 100 ACRES

be to Kinver Edge, where you could see for miles, all across to Enville and the beginning of the Sheep Walks and the wood where the secret chapel was hidden. We climbed up to the Edge past the caves where one or two families lived, and came back down at Nanny's Rock. Once we met a mole catcher below Kinver Edge and he was wearing a waistcoat made of velvety mole skins.

Ray wanted to buy a young Shire mare. I was to be allowed to go with him to Shrewsbury horse sales, held on the last Saturday of every month, provided that I behaved myself. Shrewsbury was about thirty-five miles away, but it was a large auction attracting buyers from as far afield as Wales and Derbyshire. We went by bus. At Shrewsbury Ray said, "I just want to go this way first." "To see a man about a dog, Daddy?" I asked. "No, no, to a shop." In the harness shop were glittering streams of horse brasses in an uncountable number of designs. He treated himself to a swinger and the shop keeper wrapped it in a piece of newspaper. Ray stuffed it into his pocket and strode off to the auction with me running to keep up with him.

In the yards at the auction I felt very small. The horses were enormous, as I'd known they would be, but there were so many of them, all possessing four huge hooves. It was difficult for me to know where to stand for the best to avoid Ray's saying sharply, "Watch out for the hind legs there". When I moved out of range of one, I was under the hooves of another. He was looking about him, hailing old So-and-So whom he'd last met fifteen years ago when delivering potatoes for grandfather, or bidding "How d'you do" to Mr Somebody, a real gentleman, who'd bought one of Bounce's foals.

He found a mare he seriously fancied and had her trotted out, chatted with her owner. Where did he come from? Oh yes! Perhaps you know old So-and-So from Ludlow, fancy that, I knew his brother, and didn't I see a colt of yours sold at Uttoxeter, and would you believe it, isn't it a small world, and is the mare absolutely safe in traffic?

In the sale ring the mare is a picture of equine loveliness. She has absolutely no vices, is four years old. Some idiot brandishes a stick and the mare plunges forwards. The handler hangs on and manages to keep his feet on the ground. I peer between the twill and worsted covered legs, the hob-nailed boots and leggings.

Ray stopped bidding at seventy guineas. He hadn't meant to go above sixty. She went at ninety-two guineas. He shrugged his shoulders regretfully but said "Perhaps it's just as well. I reckon she'd be a bit of a handful."

So back we went to the bus. The best of the day was over, the bustling, the shouting, the smell of horses, the knowing dealers, the quiet bargainings in corners and the suffused faces after a pint too many. At least I didn't have a problem there with my father. Half a pint of beer made him sick and put him in bed for a day with a migraine. Whisky, which he could tolerate, was too expensive to drink very often. We hurried back to the bus, Ray thinking now of the calves waiting to be fed at home and the cows that had to be milked.

It was two or three months before he again went to Shrewsbury, this time without me. He returned by train to Stourbridge Junction with a fine Shire mare, young, good-tempered and placid. He walked her home along the roads from Stourbridge. Her name was Brown and she had cost him eighty guineas.

In October 1938 Ray and Bid's third daughter, and last child, Judith, was born and she was christened at Enville Church.

Bid wrote, "We never could get rich from sunshine, gentle climate and lovely scenery, much as I loved it all. In fact that was partly the trouble – the land was too dry. It was loose and sandy and overrun by rabbits. It was heartbreaking to try to fence against them. They burrowed beneath any fence and ate everything in the garden and fields."

The average income for a farmer with a hundred acres was, at this time, £3 a week, which was very little for the times. The average size for a farm was about seventy acres. Agricultural prices were below the level they had been ten years earlier. Ray began to search for another farm. We all travelled by bus to view one near Droitwich. The house was huge and one room had a splendid marble fireplace made by someone famous, but Ray didn't like there being an unfenced canal running through some fields. Besides that the rent was really more than he wanted to pay. Sometimes Ray's father went with him to look at a farm. Eventually they found one near Lichfield, with some of its fields in Staffordshire and some in Warwickshire. That was where we would go but would that we had stayed with the rabbits and the yew at Enville! Things might have turned out differently if we had, but we will never know.

CHAPTER FIVE

Camp Farm

B id wrote, "We were able to agree definitely to take the tenancy of the new farm, which I had not seen and could only imagine from the reports of Ray and his father, and I hoped for the best. The young Agricultural College trainee who was taking Falcon Farm brought his bride-to-be to see the house and she seemed as pleased with it as I had always been." Ray reported that there was no pond at the new farm. Bid was sorry, for she was especially fond of our ducks and if there were no pond then they would not be happy there and we could not take them with us.

We moved at the end of March 1939. I had no time for sadness at leaving as I anticipated with excitement a whole new territory to explore. Ray was travelling in the cattle van with Norman Shepherd who had agreed to accompany us to Camp Farm and stay for a few weeks until things were sorted out. Bid, with Ken, Christine and the baby, together with Bid's friend Betty, travelled with the furniture, and I went in the cattle van after it returned for another load. I perched up on the passenger seat beside the driver, with Nellie at my feet, patient and well behaved as she always was.

Bid and the others arrived at the new farm before me. Bid wrote, "On descending from the van, I knew at once that this new home would never feel like the one we had left. I noticed the cold breeze, and shielding the baby in my arms I went straight into the house, my companion having gone first to unlock the doors. With a quick glance round I thought it was quite satisfactory and I was so glad Betty had come with me to direct the men with the furniture. I found we had three good bedrooms, parquet-floored front room, gas light and gas cooking stove and a long dry cellar."

Travelling along the lanes the driver of my van said: "Ain't so far now. Five or six miles to go." I craned eagerly to look out over the leafless hedges and trees, the winter fields with strips of ploughing. The landscape was flatter than round Enville but I looked forward to whatever there was to come. "There," the driver said, "it's that white place ahead."

Camp Farm was long and low. Its façade was painted white and its window frames were painted black, like sooty eyes in a clown's face. It stood sideways on to the lane and looked out over a small garden and an acre of paddock.

Nell and I climbed stiffly down and looked about us. The farmyard opened straight on to the lane and it was encircled by the rear of the house, the barn, the loose-boxes and the stables. One of the first things that struck me about the surroundings was that the countryside, even for March, was not as lush as that we had left. It was much more bare. The trees were not as plentiful, nor as tall. Of course with so much less woodland there were fewer areas to harbour the dreadful rabbit pest that Ray had come here to escape. It proved to be a windy place and Bid remarked that we ought to have taken note that Sutton Coldfield, which was only a few miles away, must have been so named for a reason.

I explored the fields that I eventually came to know so well. I found the places where special wild flowers grew and where there were sweet chestnut trees, but most of all it was the brook that ran through the Bog Field that attracted us children. It was perfect: a purling, crystal clear stream that ran

Lichfield — The first church was consecrated in 700, then there was a Norman Cathedral in 1140. This was gradually replaced with new building by 1340

Saint Chad's — During the Commonwealth Parliamentarians deliberately wrecked the Cathedral, but it was carefully restored in the 1660's.

Old terra cotta tiles in the Sacristy

over shining brown pebbles. Green weed undulated in its current, water-cress grew at its edges, along with brook-lime, king-cups, rushes, ragged robins, and all manner of marshy plants, while alders shaded its banks.

The Bog Field encompassed thirty acres of old grassland, almost a third of the acreage of the entire farm, and it was roughly divided into sections by a few ancient hawthorns, the remains of hedgerows that had long ago divided the field into the smaller pastures of Near Bogs, Middle Bogs, Far Bogs, Bogs Croft and so on. This wonderful stream and this old pasture would later prove to be the cause of our heartbreak at Camp Farm.

The village of Little Hay had no church and no school. It consisted of a few cottages and farms, a solid red brick Water Board building and a public house. I had to cycle southwards to school at Mere Green, up a hill between large fields. Then beyond an oak wood and a chicken farm, the houses began, and they continued for about fifteen miles, right through Four Oaks, Sutton Coldfield, Aston, Birmingham and through the city's southern suburbs. As I swept on my bicycle back down the hill on my way home to Camp Farm I could look way over the fields to the far horizon and see the faint silhouette there of Lichfield cathedral's three spires: the "ladies of the vale".

This school was nothing like Enville School which had almost a family atmosphere. There were no vast tables here covered with specimens of twigs, wild flowers, tadpoles, birds' feathers and dead beetles; no home-made music as Mrs Jackson had strummed it on her mandolin, singing in her cracked voice; no country dancing with the boys reluctantly hopping round in heavy boots. Mere Green was more of a town school. Girls occupied a different building from the boys. The girls' fathers were employed in a huge variety of ways and their earnings varied enormously. None of my friends were country girls here. There didn't seem to be any in the school.

Shortly after we arrived at the farm there came stalking across the fields a golden cat, full grown but still young, taut and sleek, with yellow eyes. Christine saw him first as he sauntered into the farmyard and she picked him up. He promptly scratched her and she dropped him quickly, wailing at the top of her voice. Bid gave him milk. Ray asked the neighbours if anyone had lost a handsome ginger cat but no one claimed him and so Sandy stayed. We children had the greatest respect for him. He was a stern and humourless cat, all warm colour, amber, gold and orange, on the outside, but inside he was cold and cruel. He was Bid's pet and she loved his beauty and self-reliance.

I kept a pet rabbit once, and while cleaning out its hutch I put her into a loose-box which had a small sliding panel in the top half of the door. This I left ajar. I set the hutch all clean and ready and turned to the loose-box to fetch my rabbit. As I turned I glimpsed Sandy slipping like a silk scarf down from the opening in the door. Fear nearly choked me. He wouldn't touch my rabbit, would he? Surely he wouldn't! I wrenched open the door and there lay my poor doe dead upon the straw.

"He did it just for fun!" I cried to Bid. "He didn't even want to eat her!" The cat was there too, crouching in the kitchen, as if Bid were to be the judge of the situation between us. Bid was sorry, but she couldn't bring my pet back to life again. "It's his nature to kill," was all she could say. Sandy glared hostilely at me, arrogant as a feudal king, and I glared back, and that was that. A cat was an animal which killed. I had to accept that.

Norman left to return to Enville and Ray again needed help. Nowadays labour was becoming more difficult to obtain. He could find no one locally

CAMP FARM

LITTLE HAY, LICHFIELD

Shelter Shed

Implement Shed

Harness Room

Rick Yard

Stable

Loose Box

Fold Yard

Cow Shed Loft above

Loose Box

Barn

Manure Heap

Privy

The layout of the farm was typical of those built during the late 1700's and early 1800's for a small mixed arable and livestock holding.

The buildings were planned so that in winter fodder could easily be carried in to the stock, the manure could be removed to the yard and from there it was carted to fertilise the fields to grow fodder for the following year.

MANLEY HALL, Weeford Parish, built above the pretty valley of the Blackbrook by John Shawe Manley, Esq. in 1833, and was the seat of landlord Colonel Roger Shawe Manley in 1939, but he did not occupy it.

from Manley Hall Estate Papers: CAMP FARM

Lady Day 1939, Alfred Burke, Half year rent £58·2·6
Michaelmas Day 1939, F.W. Raybould, Half year rent £45·0·0
26 Jan. 1940. F.W. Raybould, in settlement of ingoing valuation £57·6·9.

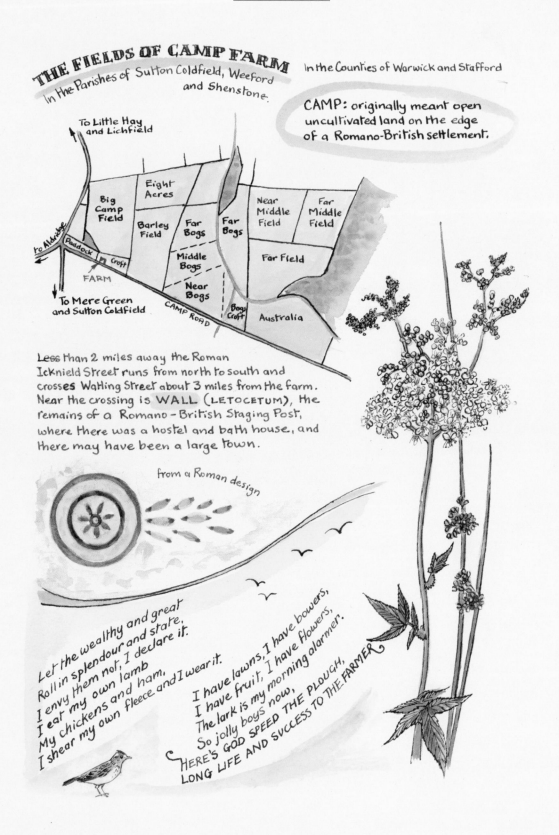

THE FIELDS OF CAMP FARM

In the Parishes of Sutton Coldfield, Weeford and Shenstone.

In the Counties of Warwick and Stafford

CAMP: originally meant open uncultivated land on the edge of a Romano-British settlement.

To Little Hay and Lichfield

To Aldridge

Big Camp Field

Eight Acres

Barley Field

Far Bogs

Far Bogs

Near Middle Field

Far Middle Field

Paddock

Croft

FARM

Middle Bogs

Far Field

To Mere Green and Sutton Coldfield

Near Bogs

CAMP ROAD

Bogs Croft

Australia

Less than 2 miles away the Roman Icknield Street runs from north to south and crosses Watling Street about 3 miles from the farm. Near the crossing is WALL (LETOCETUM), the remains of a Romano-British Staging Post, where there was a hostel and bath house, and there may have been a large town.

from a Roman design

Let the wealthy and great
Roll in splendour and state,
I envy them not, I declare it.
I eat my own lamb
My chickens and ham,
I shear my own fleece and I wear it.

I have lawns, I have bowers,
I have fruit, I have flowers,
The lark is my morning alarmer.
So jolly boys now,
HERE'S GOD SPEED THE PLOUGH,
LONG LIFE AND SUCCESS TO THE FARMER.

and so he advertised for a boy to live in and train in farming. A town boy called Patrick was delivered by car by his brother who worked for the BBC. Patrick was about fourteen years old, of an age when he had no time for young girls like me, just as I was of an age when I looked down my nose at boys, particularly townie boys. I daresay that deep down I was envious that he was on the farm all day, while I was at school. Because he lived with the family, where I had been the oldest child, there was a struggle for supremacy between us. We soon disliked each other intensely. Before long Patrick decided that the farming life was not for him, and I was heartily pleased when his brother came to retrieve him.

Over at Egg Hill, grandfather George was now in his seventies, but he had Harold, Quintin and Bob working on the farm, with occasional help from George. As Ray was so short-handed Bob came from Egg Hill to help. It was a foregone conclusion that such an arrangement would be short-lived. Bob was a volatile personality, one minute charming and full of fun, the next being thoroughly nasty to everyone. Despite everyone starting out with the best of intentions and trying very hard to keep up the good behaviour, no more than a week went by before Bob was away in a huff back to Egg Hill.

Ray had to manage as best as he could with any local short-term help that came his way. Bid did her best but did not have much time to spare. She wrote, "One of the pleasantest jobs was haymaking, when I could enjoy the sunshine and keep an eye on the children as well. One summer we had the baby (Judith) in the pram there, too. I was on the load, it was easier for me than pitching or raking. As the horse moved on the children were supposed to bring the baby along with us, but after they had forgotten twice Ray had a better idea. With a rope he hitched the pram to the wagon. The substantial old pram did not topple over but came bumpety-bump over the hard earth. Every time the horse started on with a jerk, baby came lurching behind, and many times I sat down suddenly with a plop amongst the sweet-scented hay."

Ray bought a 1932 Standard car, somewhat dilapidated, and on most Monday mornings it took him to Lichfield Market. Sometimes he would bring back a calf on the rear seat of the car with its body and legs enclosed in a sack so that it would lie quietly for the five mile journey home. Once he brought back a little red calf with a white star on her forehead which he gave to Christine and she called her Poppy. Christine learned to let the calf suck milk off her fingers out of a bucket. Another time he brought a calf which he said was a Red Poll and would never grow any horns. She hadn't been de-horned, she simply could never develop any. I had thought that all cows had horns and so this one was a real novelty. In those days, when most women wore hats, it was said that "a cow without horns was like a woman without a hat".

When there were several animals to take or to bring back from market then Ben Dobson, the drover, turned up with a lorry. Old Ben was a rough, tough, hard, beer-drinking drover, a warrior of a man with a broken nose and a lame leg. He travelled with the lorry driver, leaning forward in his seat, resting his arms upon his stick and chewing a straw. Out of the lorry, the sight of him, standing square in his big hob-nailed boots and greasy cap, waving his knobbled stick, could not fail to deter a herd of frisky bullocks from stampeding through Lichfield city.

Sometimes Old Ben's son Tom, when he could find nothing better to occupy himself with on a winter Sunday afternoon, came to Camp Farm with his ferrets and nets. Then Ken and I would accompany him down to the warrens in the Bog Field hedges. Sometimes the rabbits ran unexpectedly from un-netted burrows, then Nell chased after them, snapping at their white tails as they ran through the clumps of rushes and hawthorns.

Occasionally the ferret didn't reappear from the hole and Tom swore dreadfully, wishing he'd secured it on a long string instead of trusting it to come back of its own accord. He set to work with a spade to dig out the burrow he thought the lost ferret might be in, while Nell attacked another hole, whimpering and tearing away at soil and roots with her claws and teeth, and burying our feet under the mounds of earth she threw out from between her hind legs. "Go on Nell! Get in there, Nell!" Ken and I always hoped Nell would catch more rabbits than Tom's ferrets could, but of course she never did.

FERRETS   male = hob female = jill babies = kittens.
They enjoy bread and milk but need a high protein diet
with plenty of meat of all kinds.

On one particular Sunday afternoon Tom turned up on his bike, but without his ferrets. He had come straight from having a pint too many at The Blue Ball. The bicycle decided to take advantage of its drunken rider and kept rearing up on its hind wheel, trying to throw Tom off. Tom thought it needed a drink of water from the water trough. Ken, Christine and I congregated to watch the show, and it turned out to be fine entertainment for a dull Sunday afternoon. The bicycle didn't fancy a drink. It swerved and reared and bucked all over the yard with Tom clinging on like a rodeo rider, swearing and cussing so hard I hoped Bid wouldn't come out and hear any of it. "The bugger won't drink," Tom declared, staring despairingly at us. "But I'll make the sod drink, I will, you see if I don't!" The circus was over all too soon when the bicycle swerved sideways against the trough. It was Tom himself who took the drink as he toppled in, head first.

Most years Ray bred a foal or two. Lichfield was the headquarters of the local branch of the Shire Horse Society, to which Ray subscribed, and in the spring he was asked if he could provide board and lodging for a stallion and groom for one or two nights every three weeks or so. The stallion was led in a

from a painting
by F. Babbage

THE SHIRE STALLION
HAROLD (1881-1901)
bred by J.H. Potter
owned by A.C. Duncombe
of Calwich Abbey, Derbyshire,
was one of the most
famous Shire stallions.

By 1939 almost all the
Shire stallions in the Stud
Book were descended from
Harold.

Three distinct types of cart horse
emerged from the equine population in
the late 1800's: the Shires, the
Clydesdales and the Suffolks. Stud
books were started.
THE SHIRE BOOK BEGAN IN 1878
initiated by Mr. Frederick Street
of St. Ives, Cambs.

A shire stallion should stand
from 16½ hands to over 17, with
a wide chest, bright and kindly
eye, docile temperament, and
a short back and muscular
loins. The characteristics of
the breed are large size and
weight, giving the ability to
move heavy loads.

"If the sun shines on a stallion's
face while he is serving a mare the
foal will have four white feet."
Old Saying.

Ray and Gay Spark

circuit of about twenty miles round the countryside serving the mares of farmers as he went. The horse was already in the farmyard when I first saw him, eighteen hands of dapple grey muscle, with arched crest, and fiery eye. His groom was quite insignificant beside this glorious beast. "What's his name, please, Mister?" "Gee Spak." We translated this as "Gay Spark". The groom had a strong Scottish accent.

All spring these two walked the lanes together, around Burton-on-Trent, Coleshill, and Lichfield. All over England stallions were being walked to serve mares, not only the Shires, but the Suffolks in Eastern England and the Clydesdales in the north.

Gay Spark was housed in one of the loose-boxes, the catches to the door double-checked and the yard gate to the road kept closed. He was worth a great deal of money. The groom was not a talkative man, much to my disappointment. He ate up the dinner Bid provided for him and then sat reading a novel by Zane Grey or Nat Gould until he went to bed at nine o'clock.

In the middle of the night, during one of his visits, Ray awoke to hear a great banging and crashing coming from the yard. "What's that, Bid?" he muttered, pulling on his trousers and groping for his boots. It sounded as if a demolition gang was at work in the yard. He was a few yards outside the back door when the grey stallion loomed over him. The horse had had no trouble in kicking his way out of the loose-box, bursting the bolts off at top and bottom. Ray approached cautiously, hoping to catch him by his headstall, but the animal reared up in fright. Ray glimpsed the horse's massive belly and enormous hooves poised right above him, so he turned and ran, sprinting up the stairs and pounding on the groom's door. "Hey there, mate! Get up, get up, will yer? Yer hoss's loose and breaking the yard up!"

The groom stumbled downstairs and took things calmly. "All right, me old dearie," he said, "all right then. Come along now." The monster calmed at once. Ray, who watched from the safety of the kitchen doorway, reported afterwards, "He followed him back into the box just like an old sheep, just like an old sheep he was." In the morning Gay Spark was led out and reverently escorted to the rick yard, where Brown awaited his attentions.

Ray very rarely called in a vet. They cost money, and very often did not accomplish much for there was not even penicillin or antibiotics in those days. Like horsemen from centuries past Ray relied on his own expertise, plus an array of commercial remedies, such as Tipper's Mystery (it was a mystery how it cured anything!), Brown Chemical Extract for wounds and to smear on the arm when assisting calving, or a variety of mixtures marketed by Elliman's. A constitutional ball was the usual medicine for a horse that was a bit sluggish and off its feed. Perhaps bad winter weather had kept it standing in the stable for longer than was healthy. Constitutional balls were hard, dark brown, like liquorice and about the size of golf balls, and were supposed to be shot down the horse's throat with a "gun". Like many horsemen, Ray had never owned one of these instruments and sometimes the ball would bounce back out of the horse's throat and finish up on the floor.

He would soften the ball slightly with the warmth of his hands until it became tacky, then he impaled it onto a sharpened stick, and pushed the stick over the horse's tongue and down its throat. If all went perfectly well the ball came off the stick and went down the animal's throat and the stick was withdrawn.

One winter, when old Bounce stood listlessly, ignoring her bait, Ray decided a constitutional ball was called for. The old mare had endured many balls and drenches in her time and was generally easy to handle. Ray got her mouth open with no difficulty and pushed the stick with ball attached down her throat. He thought the ball had come off, but when he withdrew the stick he saw it was still adhering. Obviously he'd fixed it too firmly. He was holding Bounce's mouth open with one hand and he didn't want to release his grip, but he had no free hand with which to loosen the ball. He tried to free it quickly by using his teeth.

Bounce was growing impatient and beginning to slew her head about. Ray hastily took a harder grip on her nose and once more thrust the stick down her throat. This time it came back clean, but as she swallowed there was a strange cracking sound in her throat. She gave a little cough, and Ray looked down with horror, to see half of his false upper teeth lying in the manger. The

ALONG THE HEDGEROW

HEDGES: make a boundary between two different properties and prevent stock moving from one piece of land to another.

A layed hedge, after it had grown unchecked for a few years.

Warning to huntsmen: hidden wire, dangerous to jump.

hedgerow tree to provide shade for animals

old bedhead to stop up a gap

Hedges were usually "brushed" (cut back) every winter to check growth.

Hawthorn (May or Whitethorn) makes a strong, stockproof hedge.

Blackthorn, snowy white flowers come out before the leaves.

Holly, slow growing but almost impenentrable.

Hazel, useful for poles and sticks.

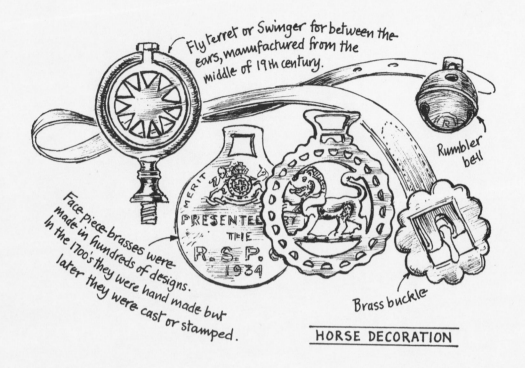

Fly terret or Swinger for between the ears, manufactured from the middle of 19th century.

Rumbler bell

Face piece brasses were made in hundreds of designs. In the 1700's they were hand made but later they were cast or stamped.

MERIT PRESENTED THE R.S.P. 1934

Brass buckle

HORSE DECORATION

realisation dawned that the whole of his top plate had gone from his mouth, and that the other half must still be stuck to the constitution ball and it was now reposing in Bounce's stomach. He rushed into the house. "Oh! Bid! Bounce's swallowed my teeth!" he cried. "Oh dear! Will they hurt her?" "I dunno. But she's in foal you know!" He said worriedly. But Bounce's sluggish condition improved and she suffered no ill-effects. Spring came, and she bore a beautiful filly foal. We watched the little filly stand shakily on splayed legs and search for Bounce's milk. "Thank goodness it hasn't been born with false teeth," Bid laughed.

One Friday early in 1941 I cycled home from school in a flurry of snowflakes. On Monday morning it was still snowing and Ray had to cut high walled corridors across the farmyard to the barn, the cowsheds and the stables. Colder days followed. The three feet of snow became encrusted with ice, lengthy icicles fringed the gutterings and the animals' whiskers, rattled at the end of the cows' tails. Fernlike patterns of frost encrusted the window panes

and hardly melted all day long. All fur and feather was puffed out for maximum warmth. Hay seeds trailed from the barn across the snow, a fragrant reminder of a far away summer. Ray spent all his time carrying feed to animals. All the beasts, even the bullocks who usually roughed it out in the fields with a supply of hay and roots, had to be brought into shelter. The horses stamped and snoozed in the stable. With no work to do and no excercise their legs swelled up. It was a condition often referred to as "Monday morning leg".

I took Bounce walking through the snow, leading her down the lane, picking our way round sculpted drifts and then wading across the Bog Field. We tried to keep to where the wind had blown the snow to a thinner, icy, covering. The ice crust was so thick that Nell could run over snow three or four feet deep with never a paw penetrating it, but Bounce's big hooves shattered the dimpled ice-layer at every step and her fetlocks were immersed in cold, pure-white snow. So were mine, for at every step it came over the tops of my wellingtons.

The Bog Field was a silent desert of white with the thin brown thread of the stream winding between ragged ice-lace edges. Bounce and Nell and I seemed to be the only living things in the whole world. We stood and stared at the sepia water rippling and winking through the snow and there was nothing else but the sound of our breathing. I pushed my hand under Bounce's mane and felt the warmth trapped under her long hair. Standing there with the dog and the old horse in the absolute silence and stillness of that winter afternoon I knew, though I was very young, that that was perfection.

We turned and plodded back through the drifts and by the time we reached the stables Bounce's legs had reduced to their normal size.

CHAPTER SIX

Visiting Egg Hill Farm

Now that we had the old Standard car we could occasionally visit Bid's relations in Redditch more easily, as well as Ray's at Frankley. At Egg Hill we leapt from the car and clattered up the alley past the pigsties to the back door where the odour of boiling potatoes that steamed for pig swill in a big iron pot wafted out in greeting. Grandma bustled to meet us along the passageway that divided the dining room from the dairy, her black hair coiled in a knot at the nape of her neck. She declared that all she used to help it keep its colour was a rinse of cold tea.

In the kitchen Grandpa sat at the table sipping tea, his booted and gaitered legs sprawled towards a bad-tempered terrier who was moored to a table leg underneath the tent-like draperies of the cloth. One step too near and the terrier would snarl and growl and was likely to have you by the ankle in an instant. To us children Grandpa seemed stern and aloof, but

once he gave me four volumes of *Livestock in Health and Disease* that contained wonderful colour plates which I often studied. I have the books still.

There was a roaring fire in the kitchen grate and joints of meat, fruit cakes and other delicacies cooking in the ovens on either side of it. Grandma's pork pies, made from pigs who had once inhabited the sties outside, were absolutely delicious, as were the lumps of chocolate waste that were passed round in big brown bags; they came from Cadbury's factory, and tasted just as good as the perfect product.

Bob was toasting bacon over the fire, its fat dripping and flaming on the coals. Arguments sparked out of Bob, restlessness galvanised his lean limbs. He teased us, made silly jokes, and to entertain us further would blink obligingly in turn first his blue eye and then his brown eye. Bob was a madcap. Once he fired his shotgun up the chimney to clear the soot.

All our uncles were smallish men who wore flat caps and hob-nailed boots, and talked at the tops of their voices, waving their arms about and cussing about this and that. Quintin was, perhaps, the quietest of the brothers. He kept bees, liked gardening, tended the pigs. "Eats just like pigs, don't they?" he laughed, pouring the swill into the pigs' troughs. They kept about fifteen pigs at Egg Hill, about thirty head of cattle and four working horses.

George was often at the farm, although he was married now to lively Doris Edwards and lived with little Norma down the lane in the cottage where I had been born. The rumour was that as a baby Norma was always washed in milk. Maybe it was the milk that was left over from the milkround business that George was building up.

Harold sat undoing his leggings, telling a tale: "Nearly got me in the corner, the bugger did." His voice rose, his eyes grew round with the remembered danger. "I thought I was a goner, I can tell you! I leapt over the door like a bloody flea! The bugger ripped me trousers from thigh to knee," he waved his arms about, "and quiet as a lamb he'd been for weeks." "I dunno, Harold," George broke in, "it was only a month ago that the bugger had a go at me in the field. If the gate hadn't been right behind me I'd have had it, sure as eggs is eggs! You never can trust a bull," George went on, "turn on you quick as looking, and after you've been with 'em for years, an' all." "You had to laugh, though," Harold quickly changed from indignation to mirth, slapping his hands on his knees. "That time when we'd been hedging. The bloody old fool charged across the field and stood in the ash of the bonfire. Started bellowing and pawing all the soot and cinders up in clouds. Covered hisself in blacks, he did, the silly old bugger."

We heard the local news. Grandma was a lively conversationalist: "Do you remember so-and-so? Dropped down dead last week in Rubery! . . . they've chopped down all those trees now, y'know . . the old dog's on his last legs . . .

you know Mrs What's-her-name, she's in a really bad way . . .". To children's questions she had the infuriating stock replies. "How old are you, Grandma?" "As old as my tongue and a bit older than my teeth." "Do come for a walk, Grandma." "Not now. I've got a bone in my leg."

Ray liked to catch up with the news but he was always pleased to be on the way home again, back to his cows who were always waiting to be milked. Egg Hill brought back many harsh memories. "Your Dad worked too hard ever to have time for any proper fun," Bid said. "He never played football, or anything, like other boys did." "But he had a pony," I pointed out. "That was my only bit of pleasure," Ray replied. "Egg Hill was a slave house."

Rose Hips, rich in Vitamin C, were collected to send away for making Rose Hip syrup.

CHAPTER SEVEN

Wartime

On 3 September 1939 war was declared against Germany. Bid wrote, "Soon we acquired a wireless set, and it informed us that we were at war with Germany again, in spite of having, not long ago, won the 'war to end all wars'. It was frightening to hear the soon-to-be-well-known drone of a German aeroplane above your head while you were out blackberrying with the children, and wondering where its load of bombs was destined for."

At first nothing much happened after war was declared and it was months before air raids began over the Midlands. Ray constructed an air raid shelter underneath the corner of a hay stack but we were all nervous in it. The stack above us was held up on planks supported by wooden posts and Ray's theory was that, if a bomb should fall, its blast would be cushioned by the hay. Bid and I couldn't help but think of all that hay on top of us and what would happen if the posts gave way, or if they dropped an incendiary and the stack caught fire.

We cowered in the hay cave and listened to the whines and bangs of bombs being dropped round about and to the throbbing drone of the aeroplanes. "Is that one of ours, Daddy?" Ken would anxiously ask. "Yes, dear," Bid would answer. "Sounds like a Jerry to me," Ray would reply, with the lack of tact that was common to members of his family.

Bid wrote, "It was rarely the bombs were unloaded right out in an unpopulated country area, though sometimes they consisted of incendiaries which would be released to set fire to a farm or fields of corn. More often the bombers were making their way to the busy industrial cities and we found that our new farm was surrounded by important manufacturing centres. From these we heard the bombs exploding and saw flames from the areas of fire they caused."

The night sky was always brilliant with the criss-cross beams of searchlights scraping and probing amongst the stars for the flash of a wing with a black cross upon it. The searchlights were comforting to see. At last the All Clear siren penetrated every corner of the countryside with loud relief

Searchlights

and we hurried back to cocoa and the comfort of aluminium hot water bottles in knitted covers.

Over the winter the hay was fed to the cattle and then Ray dug out a shelter in the ground, covered with corrugated iron sheets, wood and earth. We flitted to it across the rick yard in the moonlight, while the animals sensibly slept in their stalls. Ray clutched the lamp off a bicycle, which, of course, couldn't be switched on until we were closed up in the hole in case the German pilots should spot the light. The dug-out was damp, it smelled of stagnant water, there were beetles and worms, Judith cried, Ray had stepped in a cow pat as he ran across the yard in just his socks, Bid thought there might be a rat, and tempers were shortened by tiredness. Perhaps the hay cave had not been such a bad idea after all for at least it had smelled good. Ray heard of one hay stack that had been bombed. Sheep had been sheltering on one side of it and none had been injured.

On the night of 14 November 1940 the whole of the sky to the south-west glowed pink. We remembered the northern lights we had seen at Enville, but this time the sky was red from fire. Next day we heard that Coventry had been destroyed, the cathedral was burned to a shell and people had fled from the fires in the city.

As the air raids over the Birmingham area became more frequent people escaped in the evenings out of the built-up areas to the nearest patch of countryside they could find. Our farm was one of the first they came to as they escaped to the north-west. Bid wrote, "We heard of many people driving into country lanes to spend a night in their cars rather than stay sleepless in their homes in town. One family with two small boys called to ask if we could let them have a bedroom, and we were glad to fix them up. Every evening they arrived by car and were happy to get a peaceful night. Shortly they were asking if they could stay during the day time as well, so we let them have our large drawing room and the use of the kitchen. We had no bathroom. The husband was a butcher and when the shop was closed on Wednesdays they would all go off to their home to get provisions and have baths . . . One night each week the butcher had to stay in town to take his turn at fire-watching, and then his lady assistant came to our house and was grateful for one night's sleep."

Winter Colour: Twigs decorated with pink crepe paper "almond blossom"

THE PIANOLA

Oats wrapped in silver paper

This family, the Goughs, came from Handsworth, and Bid was always pleased afterwards to be able to say that she and Mrs Gough never once had any dispute over sharing the kitchen. Bid was not very keen to accommodate also Mrs Gough's mother, her bed and her pianola, but somehow they were all squeezed into the drawing room and the bedroom. Mrs Gough told me that I was welcome to play the pianola whenever I liked and as there were many pianola rolls of music to go through I was kept entertained on many wet afternoons. The little boys, Brian and David, ran about the farm with Ken, Christine and Judith.

When Nell gave birth to six puppies, one puppy was adopted by each child

THE FARMYARD FOWL were often hybrids.

SOME POPULAR BREEDS

WYANDOTTE and ORPINGTON } Both general purpose fowl, good as table birds, layers and sitters, making good mothers. Eggs brown.

RHODE ISLAND RED — brown eggs and LEGHORN — white eggs } Both good layers but bad sitters.

INDIAN GAME — Good table bird with fleshy breast. Good for crossing.

MINORCA — A hardy bird. A good layer of white eggs, poor sitter.

A hen could lay about 130 eggs a year, but few in winter.

EGGS EGGS

Leghorn Cock

Orpington Cock

RIDDLE:

In marble walls as white as milk
Lined with a skin as soft as silk;
Within a fountain crystal clear
A golden apple doth appear.
No doors there are to this stronghold
Yet thieves break in and steal the gold —

F·R·M·

REGULAR MEALS

Eggs, bacon, fried bread

DINNER

Roast meat (Sundays)
Stew and dumplings
Liver, Cottage Pie,
all with potatoes and
vegetables in season

Fruit pie, Stewed fruit, Suet,
Rice, Tapioca or Bread Pudding
most with Custard

TEA

Bread and butter with
Marmite, dripping, jam, and
pickled damsons (sometimes)

Cake: sponge, fruit, caraway
seed, oat cake or fairy cakes.
Tinned fruit, jelly or
blancmange (Sundays)

FROM BID'S RECIPE BOOK

Haddock Smoked
Trim off tail & fins. Put in pan and
cover with cold water. Bring to boil.
As soon as it boils, put lid on and
remove pan from heat. Leave for 5 to
10 mins when it will be done & tender.
(You hope!)

MR. CHAD ? CHALKED ON
BUILDINGS
IN WARTIME.
WOT! NO
ORANGES?

¼ lb. Butter or Margerine
¼ lb. Sugar
½ lb. Quaker Oats
1 Teasp. Almond Essence

OAT CAKE
Dissolve sugar & butter
in saucepan
Stir in essence and oats.
Mix well.
Press into greased tin.
Bake ½ hour, in slow oven at 170°C 325°F
Ease from sides of tin while still warm

SUPPER

Bread, cheese, pickled
onions. Cooked meat or
pork pie (occasionally).
Tea (with a dash of whisky).
Biscuits and Ovaltine.

on the understanding that it was only until such time as they would be found new homes. One was to be kept, and he, of course, I named Jock after the pup I had lost at Enville. Little David Gough, a gentle and quiet four-year-old, had the smallest, an all-white puppy, whom we called Nance. "Where's David?" Someone would ask. "In the barn, with his puppy," was the invariable reply. One by one the puppies went to new homes. Nance was the last to leave. David gulped back the tears. "You can play with Jock any time," I told him, and he went away pale-faced to console himself by digging a hole in the garden.

Bid wrote, "Meanwhile we had many requests for permission to bring a caravan into a field as sleeping quarters for a family and Ray turned no one away without good cause as long as there was space, because he was sorry for them. One morning one family with three schoolboys had gone off to their work and schools as usual and we were surprised when they returned later the same morning. They had found their lovely home lying as rubble in the garden, so they made the best of life in the caravan."

By now we had given up going out to our air raid shelter. Bid said, "All these folk think it's much safer here than in town, so what are we running to the shelter for? We might just as well stay in the house and hope for the best." And so we did, sitting up fearfully in our beds, or downstairs by the embers of the fire, listening to the droning planes and bits of shrapnel falling against the window panes beyond the thick black-out curtains. On really bad nights people from the caravans felt more secure within bricks and mortar, and being together with other people helped, so they came in too, to sleep on our living room floor and make themselves cups of tea.

Sometimes, on a Sunday, when Ray had finished the morning milking and he had sufficient petrol, we would go in the Standard through Birmingham to Redditch to see if Bid's family were all right. Ray would drive past the silver barrage balloons that were tethered at Five Ways and then across scarred and pitted Birmingham. I glimpsed a man in Edgbaston standing on the doorstep of a large house and crying openly where anyone could see him. Next door there was only half a house. Grandma in Redditch was always all right, although on some visits we were obliged to descend to her cellar while there was a raid.

Over at Frankley they were also experiencing bombs. Cousin Norma at Egg Hill Cottage was about six years old. She remembered, "One Wednesday afternoon, the date of which I cannot recall, I was down the fields with Uncle Quint and Uncle Bob when I saw the balloons over Birmingham disappear, with what looked like little bees passing between them. I then recognised the familiar sound of a German aircraft and no less than five bombs fell on the farm that afternoon . . . We were next to Shed Field and as one dropped it bounced us out of the kale in which we were hiding. Thankfully it did not go off . . . Grandpa was convinced they were after his cattle. I can see Grandma and Uncle Harold now, running and crying because they thought I had been killed.

"Then came the afternoon when the balloon opposite the cottage was hit by enemy aircraft and I was in the cottage alone, as my parents were outside. The wire cut the chimneys off like a knife through butter. Mother escaped death by inches as she ran to the house as the chimneys were falling; and in fact they fell straight through the garage and flattened a van therein."

There was a smith in most villages. He worked with iron — repairing machinery, shoeing horses, making gates, railings, and tools of all kinds.

THE BLACKSMITH

"And he fighteth with the heat of the furnace: The noise of the hammer and anvil is ever in his ears, And his eyes look still upon the pattern of the thing that he maketh; He setteth his mind to finish his work, And watcheth to polish it perfectly."
Apocrypha - Ecclesiasticus 38

THE HOOF

heel
bar
sole
frog

Blood vessels in the foot are well protected by horny layers

nails – about 3 inches long for a cart horse

one front clip on a fore shoe, two on a hind

each shoe is individually fashioned to fit.

THE SHOE

During the war nine high explosive
bombs were dropped at Selly Oak near
Middle Park Farm, where Ray's
grandfather and Uncle Walter had
lived, and the farm was so
damaged that after the war
it was demolished.

Eventually the District
Council concerned themselves

Teaching a calf to drink.

with the caravans at Camp Farm. Bid wrote, "The District Council gave us
notice to have the caravans removed. The occupants were upset and lodged an
appeal. A court case ensued. I was designated to attend the court as Ray
(purposely) was too busy to go. I did not know what to expect but I answered all
the questions asked relating to hygiene, fresh water supply, length of stay and
price charged – which was two shillings weekly – from which the court could
conclude that we were not exactly making a living from the caravan rents. We
won the case and the caravans stayed for the time being, but the Council was
annoyed and the affair may have had some bearing on future events."

The routine work on the farm continued as always: the hedging and
ditching, the muck and lime spreading, the ploughing, the sowing, the
singling, the harvesting, the threshing. Every day there was milking at
morning and evening, cutting chaff, feeding the stock. Despite the
strangeness of war, the affairs of the natural world were comfortingly normal:
the lapwings still flew in the Barley Field, nesting on the ground there, so
that Ray was obliged to halt the horses when he spied a nest. He would move
the eggs aside and replace them after the cultivator had gone over the area.
There were still calves brought back from Lichfield market on the back seat of
the car. Decanted into the yard they would stand on unsteady legs looking at
us with innocent fringed eyes. They would eagerly suck from our fingers held
in a bucket of milk, until it seemed our fingers would be sucked right off our
hands and be swallowed down their muscular throats.

Now and again we visited the blacksmith at Weeford. Our blacksmith,

Mr Russell, was a man who always began talking at the same time as he pumped the bellows and the noise made his actual words unintelligible. One could only nod or smile in reply and hope the response was appropriate. The blacksmith was popular when the weather was wet, which made outside work unattractive. Then the horses would stand steaming outside his shop covered in sacks to give them some protection from the driving rain. How one's heart would sink when the smith took up a long straight bar, because that meant he hadn't any half-made shoes and would have to start from the beginning. That would mean waiting a full hour and a half for a complete set for one horse. The twenty-year-old postcards pinned round the door frame had already been well studied on previous visits, the routine of making the shoes was well known, too, so there was nothing for it but to wait patiently.

By now my first pony, Dolly, had been sold. Ray had bought three riding horses, Mist, Molly and Irish, with two of their foals. He sometimes hired the mares out for hacking and he intended to breed again from them. We now had a Shire mare who was called Dolly too, like my former skittish pony. One day, as the blacksmith trimmed Dolly's left fore, he remarked, "I've got a pony as you could borrow." Dolly was facing the doors, with her fore hoof perched high on a three-legged stand. She looked like a model for a bronze war charger. She arched her neck over the smith as he drew his file round the hoof, underneath the raw edges of the nails before he hammered them down. Dolly nipped her teeth into his cap, picked it off his head and flung it onto the floor. "Hold up, yer silly old woman! Here, keep her bloody head up, will yer!" "What pony's that, then?" Ray asked. "One as I've had in the family for God knows how long. Oldish, he is, but strong. Would suit your wench a treat. I'll lend him for as long as you want him. Only eating his head off here."

Tommy was a good-looking dun pony with a black mane and tail but there were two odd things about him. It's said that one should never look a gift horse in the mouth, and this was true of Tommy. We had to accept, firstly, that his owner, a blacksmith, refused to shoe him, saying he didn't need shoes. This struck me as being most contrary. His other idiosyncrasy was more annoying. He always had either to be led or to follow another horse because he would never, ever, walk ahead. Experienced riders saw Tommy as a challenge, trying everything they could think of to urge him to go in front, but he dug his unshod hooves into the ground and absolutely refused to allow his nose to be edged past the girth of the horse ahead. In the end we had to humour him. It seemed cruel to keep on trying to force him, after all he wasn't young. Even out grazing in the field he would follow one of the other horses about like a well trained dog always walking to heel. We had a lot of fun with the horses, the people who came to ride and those from the caravans too.

Nell's puppy, Jock, was growing into a beautiful dog, with a shining black coat, tan muzzle, eyebrows and legs. I loved to see him spring in the mowing grass or the wheat, great standing jumps with his ears flying up, his black mouth stretched in a grin of delight, with his eyes sharp for a mouse or rabbit that might scuttle between the stalks.

I was sad, though, because Jock had divided loyalties. Whilst he spent the weekdays with us about the farm, on a Friday afternoon he was waiting for one particular caravan occupant to arrive. Wilhelm Giesen was an elderly man, heavy, with pendulous jowls and short bowed legs, accompanied by a lady whom he confessed to Ray was not his wife.

Willy became a regular part of our weekends as well as of our dog's. His brother owned a business which printed greeting cards and Willy would bring us presents of propelling pencils, pads of drawing paper and books full of old Christmas card samples which had been discarded from the factory. He would inspect the little paintings I had executed during the week and make encouraging remarks. We all liked him. Bid said she thought he was a bit of a rogue, and that he was Jewish.

As the bombing raids over the Midlands became fewer, the townspeople relaxed. The Gough family left our front room and returned to Handsworth, and many left their caravans closed up for weeks on end without visiting them. Willy and his lady friend, however, still came regularly, enjoying their weekends in the countryside.

As things turned out, it was just as well for Jock that he had made such a good friend of Willy, for our days at Camp Farm were numbered.

A RIDGING PLOUGH

CHAPTER EIGHT

The Men from the Ministry

The war changed everyone's lives, and farmers were no exception. From the end of the previous war until the beginning of this one they had struggled through the depression, eking out a living as best as they could, with the government taking very little interest in their activities. Everywhere the farms were run down through lack of money, with buildings, drains, and fences in need of repair all over the country.

Our lives, too, were soon to take a different course and it was to be the thirty acres of marshy Bog Field that would ultimately be the reason for this change. The field was old pasture. The grass was short and sweet, mixed with herbs of all sorts and of such a variety that it must have taken a great many years for them to become established. Lapwings soared over the field and skylarks hovered above it on tremolo wings. The clear purling stream that ran beneath the alder trees for the length of the field rippled over smooth brown pebbles between which grew bunches of emerald weed that flowed and waved in the current like the green hair of a water nymph. At the edges were lush mats of watercress, brook lime and king-cups. There were always horses or cattle grazing in the field. Near the gate Ray set a pink lump of iodised rock salt and their tongues sculpted it into smooth concavities. It seemed that the Bog Field could never alter.

The war forced the government to take drastic steps to improve the state of the land because at that time 70 per cent of food for the people was imported. The war meant that few imports would be arriving and Britain must grow its own food in order to prevent the population from starving. All farmers, smallholders and market gardeners suddenly found themselves under scrutiny. As early as 1936 the government had been making plans in case there should be a war. Despite objections from some ministers that the policy of intervention was not the right one and that other methods could be found to induce the farmers to grow more food, the government decided to set up county Agricultural Committees similar to those of the First World War, whose task would be to coerce the farmers into greater production. Men from each county were selected by the government to act as the chief executives of these Committees.

The executives were free to nominate their own committees. Unfortunately this created opportunities for favouritism and nepotism, for no one on the committees was elected democratically by any body of people. At first little consideration was given to these aspects but as time went on they occasionally became apparent. J. Wentworth Day, a Cambridgeshire writer on country matters, included a blistering nineteen-page chapter entitled "Little Hitlers on the Farms" in his book *Harvest Adventure*. He was concerned at the manner in which the Committees had been formed in 1939, in a way which he considered very un-English, with the men on them "able to flaunt authority, use petrol, and order their neighbours about". As the county Chairmen and Chief Executives were free to choose friends and acquaintances to sit on their committees they were obviously not democratically chosen, but, most importantly, they were empowered to exercise Defence Regulation 62 whenever they wished. This regulation gave these Committees the right to take possession of any land together with buildings on that land, but owners and tenants who protested had no recourse to normal lawful judgment. The time-honoured ancient words of the Magna Carta, the cornerstone of English liberty, were now disregarded and a land holder no longer had the right to be tried in open court or to appeal if he were ordered to quit by these men.

Like all farmers Ray was aware that with the coming of war conditions would change. For a start there was the rationing of artificial fertilisers, animal foodstuffs and petrol, to say nothing of the rationing of food and clothing for the human population. Bid received extra sugar at jam-making time, but still she hoarded some if she could from the usual ration. Unlike town people we had our own milk, eggs and vegetables, but sometimes other foodstuffs were difficult to come by. As Bid had always been very thrifty, clothes did not present a problem as they did for some people. We did not need to look smart. My clothes were passed down to me from an older cousin in town, old woollen jumpers were unravelled and the wool that was good was knitted up again to make something else, everything was darned and darned again and nothing was thrown away until it was absolutely threadbare. Even then the rags were used for dusters and polishing cloths. Bid was occasionally left with clothes coupons that she could sell.

At first Ray did not think very much about how farming itself might

To save paper in wartime tins had small labels

Meat safe, with perforated zinc door

change or about the Committee men and how they had been selected. Then the men from the War Agricultural Committees began to visit the farms all over the country and to issue orders. Everyone called them the War Ag. The farmers knew that more food had to be produced and that they must co-operate, but sometimes they felt it was very difficult for them to do so. There were cases of dairy farmers being instructed to sell off the herds that had taken them years to build up and to plant their fields with corn or potatoes, while arable farmers who knew very well what crops would grow best on their land were irritated when ordered by a stranger who made only a brief visit to grow something they considered to be unsuitable.

Another writer, George Henderson, who ran an Oxfordshire farm in an extremely efficient manner, wrote in *The Farming Ladder* of his annoyance at orders compelling him to carry out cultivations with which he, knowing his farm so much better than an outsider, could not always agree. He said, "While no one can doubt that the vast majority of decisions are made honestly and fairly, it is a negation of British justice that there is no appeal." He felt that "The practice of forming decisions from a casual inspection of farms is unfair."

Eventually a Warwickshire War Ag. man came to see Camp Farm and he instructed Ray to plough two grass fields and to plant them with corn. Ray pointed out that the field called Australia was very poor and covered with stones and would not produce a good crop. They agreed that this year it would be better to plough Near Middle Field instead although it was smaller than Australia.

Over at Egg Hill Farm Grandpa and the uncles received specific orders for the cultivation of fifty-six of their acres, while back at Enville seventy acres of the Sheepwalks were to be ploughed and reseeded at a cost to the Estate of between £600 and £700. Enville Hall itself was eventually occupied by American troops.

Many farmers disputed their cultivation orders. Mr Pickering, in the Rugby area told the Warwickshire War Ag. that he was not in a financial position to plough fields as he had been instructed. He suggested that the

MAF 80/2921

E 1261

CLOSED UNTIL 1990

MAF 80/2921

NATIONAL AIR RAID PRECAUTIONS ANIMALS COMMITTEE, dealt with animals injured by air raids. Any killed by enemy action but which were suitable for human consumption had to be bled and disembowelled by a butcher or by the farmer himself

In 1940 the total head of cattle in Warwickshire was 143,000

There were 49 prosecutions to July 1940 in Warwickshire for failing to carry out cultivation orders. Total fines = £1,477

Committee took them over at a fair rent for the duration of the war. His offer was declined and he was informed that there were credit facilities available for causes of this kind.

At their regular weekly meetings the War Ag. Committees discussed all manner of subjects relating to their efforts to increase the acreage under plough and the production of food. They noted the letters received from disconsolate recipients of ploughing and cultivation orders and they frequently displayed utter indifference to any that pleaded hardship. In January 1941 the vicar of Eckington sent a letter to the Worcestershire War Ag. stating that Mr Griffiths of Court End Farm, Eckington was

During the 1914/18 War tractors began to be used on farms but they were unreliable, heavy, and they compacted the earth.

Pneumatic rubber tyres were introduced in 1932. By 1939 there were about 50,000 tractors in the country.

Popular makes: Fordson, Chase, Ferguson, Allis Chalmers, Massey-Harris, John Deere, International Harvester.

A 1916-28 Clayton crawler-type tractor imprinted horse-shoe shapes from its track onto the ground.

THE TRACTOR

dying and he asked whether the Committee could see its way to postponing the operation of the cultivation order which had been served on Mr Griffiths. The meeting "resolved that its previous decision be adhered to".

Between the wars thousands of men had given up farm labouring and had moved to work in towns. Ray had discovered how difficult it was to obtain help. Now that millions of extra acres had to be cultivated there were even fewer men to carry out the work as so many more had been called up to the armed forces. The farmers themselves were exempt from the call-up and often their sons and key workers were able to obtain exemption, but still there was never sufficient farm labour. At the War Ag. meetings they sometimes approved leave of absence for certain men from the armed forces so that they could help on the farms at busy times. They might discuss applications for Jewish refugee labour and the deployment of Land Girls. They granted exemptions to farm workers from Home Guard Service. Ray could not, of course, spend time in the Home Guard or nights on fire-watching duty as he was single-handed on the farm and his work had priority.

At the meetings the pest officer usually submitted a report stating the numbers of rats, rabbits, moles and foxes that had been killed and that he had sold a certain number of rabbits at one shilling and sixpence each.

An executive officer was despatched from the Warwickshire War Ag. to the Manley Estate, which included our Camp Farm fields, to view damage caused to the crops by pheasants because someone had complained. The owner of the shoot on the Estate was not slow to point out that the Committee had refused his application for petrol which meant that he could not travel to shoot the pheasants. However, the officer reported that he could find little damage caused by the pheasants to the crops.

The War Ag. decided upon the rations of artificial fertiliser, animal and poultry feed and petrol, all of which were in very short supply. Much as he loved his horses machines fascinated Ray. "Here, what d'you think of this?" he asked one day, ushering us into the fold yard. We were confronted by an ancient rusty tractor. "It reminds me of an angry old turkey cock," Bid said. She thought the machine was a waste of money. It had an intractable air and looked unreliable, which was what it turned out to be. Ray obtained a ration of fuel for it and spent time he could not afford, but nevertheless enjoyed, tinkering with it. Now and again he managed to coax it into life. It was very temperamental and rarely went out into the fields. In any case his machinery was not adapted for hitching to a tractor. His regular petrol ration was used in journeys to market where he picked up all the local news. He would return home with such information as, "Old What's-His-Name has had some of his cows blinded by shrapnel." "How does that happen, Daddy?" "Well, when there's an air raid and the cows hear an explosion in the sky or they see a light they look up and bits fall into their eyes." These cattle were sold off cheaply at market.

Ray once had a frightening experience which was caused by our own aircraft. He was ploughing with Brown and Dolly on Far Middle Field when a couple of pilots out on patrol thought they would have some fun. Their aeroplanes suddenly zoomed from over the trees and swooped low over the horses. The terrified team bolted at full gallop across the field towing the plough with Ray hanging on to the lines behind them. Shivering with fear, the horses halted at the hedge where Ray, who was bruised and furious, tried to calm them down. He inspected them for injury and fortunately there was nothing seriously wrong but that evening Bid wrote a strong letter of complaint to the Air Ministry. After some weeks a note of apology did come back from them.

Ray came back from market one day with a tale about a respectable local gentleman who, one night, had slaughtered a black-market pig in his barn. Breeders were permitted to kill only two pigs a year under licence. A crack of light had been showing through the barn doors and a policeman approached to warn whoever was inside about the black-out regulations. Hearing steps outside, the gentleman and his helpers guiltily pushed the butchered pig underneath mounds of hay. It was well hidden, and the policeman merely told them to black out the crack of light and went his way. "Well," Ray finished, laughing. "When they come to eat the meat it was full of hay seeds and no amount of washing, brushing and picking them out did any good. They couldn't get rid of them by any means! Every mouthful had hay seeds in it."

At market he heard of other farmers' experiences with the War Ag., the fields they must plough, the acres they must sow, but in the early years of the war he did not hear of the worst aspects of the compulsory powers.

The War Ag. Committees were answerable only to Robert Spear Hudson, the Minister of Agriculture under Prime Minister Winston Churchill. The

POTATO DIGGER

When in gear the rear wheel and the forks spun round as the machine moved forwards.

the blade sheared off the ridge

rotating forks dug the potatoes and threw them out

men on the Committees were his spokesmen and they were above the powers of the law. A farmer who felt himself ill done by or wronged by the War Ag. could not appeal for justice in the Law Courts. Normal British justice was denied him. While the War Ag. had a difficult task in making rapid improvements to agriculture, it was invested with power which was open to abuse. If a farmer objected that the work he had been instructed to do was completely impractical, and refused to carry out the orders, then the War Ag. exercised its ultimate power. He would be ordered to quit his farm.

Bid wrote, "We knew all about the War Agricultural Executive Committee created during the First World War and recreated during the Second. It was organised for different counties to see that farmers were doing all that they could to cultivate their land for the good of the country, to 'Dig for Victory', and to make the most of the acres under their control. We knew also that those farmers who refused for any reason to obey the instructions of their County War Ag. were simply told to get out, with no compensation, whether the land was their own, or a tenancy."

In Warwickshire the Committee meetings regularly began with a list of farmers who were in danger of being dispossessed of their farms. The National Farmers Union tried to help some individuals who found themselves at odds with the War Ag., as in the case of Mr T.R. Campion of Haseley Green. The Union sent a deputation to a Warwickshire meeting at Leamington Spa to plead his case because he had carried out all the orders issued by the Committee and yet his tenancy was to be terminated. The chairman replied

Notes from the

WARWICKSHIRE RECORDS

Romney: a long-wool sheep from pre-medieval times.

Evacuation of Romney Marsh Sheep

In June 1940 some 2,637 sheep were evacuated by train from Romney Marsh in Kent, to be agisted on farms in the Shuckborough District and at Ilmington and Shipston-on-Stour. In September they were sold at market in Rugby, Banbury and Stratford-on-Avon.

1 May 1942 MEMORANDUM
SOAP for EXECUTIVE OFFICERS

(a) Toilet Soap – One tablet for each officer at intervals of 10 weeks
(b) Cleaning Soap and Powders – 16 ozs (nominal) per week for each 10,000 sq. ft. (gross) of accommodation.

Circular from Ministry of Agriculture and Fisheries.
BINDER TWINE FOR 1941 HARVEST

Some farmers supplied their own twine when the Ministry's binders were lent to them. This left twine which the Ministry had supplied to the Committees for use in these binders in the hands of the War Ag. men. The Ministry directed that in no circumstances should this surplus twine be disposed of by the Committees themselves and the Ministry should dispose of it through the normal trade channels.

3 Sept. 1940 3184 farms, out of 3769, in the county, had been surveyed for the National Farm Survey.

Ettington Park. "This farm is infested with rabbits, to which the Committee desire the attention of the Rabbit Officer to be drawn."

RATS

KILL THE RATS NOW
An urgent appeal to farmers
STARVE THE RATS
KEEP OUT THE RATS
POISON THE RAT
TRAP THAT RAT
GAS THEM IN THE HEDGES
ORGANISE A RAT HUNT

RATS DO HITLER'S WORK

that it was impossible to consider the matter and that the original order to terminate the tenancy must stand.

The City of Birmingham had a Committee which was separate from that of Warwickshire. Its chairman was Alderman Quinney, now very elderly, the very same man who had written a reference for Ray when he had been about to part company with his father at Egg Hill and start up on his own. The task of the Birmingham Committee was to see that about 15,000 acres of playing fields, gardens, waste land, building plots and so on were ploughed and producing food. Mr Quinney and his colleagues encountered such resistance from the Council and other landowners that they could not operate and in October 1940 they resigned *en bloc*. Strangely, the Birmingham War Ag. did not use its power to dispossess, but perhaps this would have been difficult with a city council.

Other War Ag. Committees had little hesitation in throwing farmers out. The tragic case of Mr George Walden of Itchen Stoke in Hampshire was reported in a national newspaper. Mr Walden was a 65-year-old bachelor, a well respected man, but somewhat set in his ways. His father had farmed the land at Itchen Stoke before him. When the Hampshire War Ag. men instructed him to plough up four acres he flatly refused to do so. A nightmare developed.

The War Ag. arranged to have him evicted on 22 July 1940. On the appointed day he locked himself in his farmhouse. The police broke in but they could see that Mr Walden had a double-barrelled shotgun and was prepared to defend himself and his home with it, so they retreated. Mr Walden fired one barrel from the gun and one of the policemen was hit in the legs and arm with nineteen pellets. The day wore on with Mr Walden still locked in his house and policemen outside lying full length between rows of potatoes and peering through the sights of their rifles. Chickens pecked around them and an old sow waddled about. As evening came the cows bellowed in pain as their udders were distended with milk and Mr Walden was unable to milk them.

At about midnight ten armed policemen surrounded the house and threw tear gas cannisters inside but Mr Walden put on his gas mask and fired through the doorway, slightly wounding three more policemen. Several hours went by but Mr Walden would not surrender. The police forced their way in but Mr Walden still threatened them with his gun. The police shot him in the head and he died from a bullet which went through his right eye. The siege had lasted from 11.30 a.m. until about 7 a.m. the following day. All over the ploughing up of just four acres!

CHAPTER NINE

Plough the Marsh

The year 1942 did not begin well. Ray unlatched the stable door to take in the morning bait and water to the horses but, lying down on the threshold, blocking the doorway, was Bounce. "Get up, get up there, old girl!" But Bounce couldn't get up. She had somehow freed herself from her headstall and moved to the doorway, where she had fallen down. She wasn't ill, she was simply old and worn out. There was nothing that could be done for her.

With Bounce blocking the doorway Ray could not easily enter the stable to feed the other horses and he could not lead them out past her. The answer to his problem was to use the ancient 'turkey-cock' tractor. He managed to coax it to start and drove it into the yard. He fixed chains and ropes about the recumbent old mare and dragged her from the doorway into the farmyard. She made no attempt to stand. Her days were done. Ray mixed her last feed and she ate it there, lying in the frosty yard, still not making the slightest attempt to stand. Ray summoned the knacker.

I stayed in the house when he came, but Ken and Christine saw her die. They came running in and said, "Bounce is dead now. We saw her shot." They were quite unaffected, but they did not remember the early days as I did. Bounce had always been there, right from Ray's first day at Falcon Farm, a faithful servant, almost one of the family. Her going was like the end of an era, and so, in a way, it was.

Bounce would be missed. Ray could not manage without her even though during her latter months she had been used only for light work. It was imperative to buy another horse. He went up to Derby horse sales and it was about tea-time when a lorry drew up at the gate. Down the ramp Ray led a big bay mare, with black mane and tail. We all congregated to inspect her as Ray led her round the yard.

"Name of Lady le Queen," he said. "She was the best there today – a good pedigree. She's in the stud book." "What a ridiculous name." Bid said, as he led her into Bounce's old stall in the stable. "What a mouthful for a horse!"

There were fewer good horses for sale at present, with fewer foals being born because a great many fine stallions had been sent for slaughter. With so much pasture now under plough there was less grass for them and foodstuffs were heavily rationed. There was simply not sufficient fodder to feed them. Yet most farmwork was still carried out by horses and the tractors that were in use during the war generally assisted the horse power on the farms.

With so many fit men called into the forces it had become more and more difficult to find help. Ray had to do the work himself as best as he could. He was always a very energetic man who worked all the hours of the day, but a hundred acres often needed an extra pair of hands. Ray carried out all the work that the War Ag. men required of him but, on 23 October 1942, the chairman of the Warwickshire branch, Mr Herbert Wilson Hughes, together with three others, arrived to inspect Camp Farm. They looked at the ricks in the yard, ran soil through their fingers, asked about the stock and gazed with great disapproval at the thirty marshy acres of the Bog Field. "That will have to be ploughed," they said. Ray pointed out that it was too wet to plough. "It will have to be drained," they said. Ray stared in disbelief. "But that would cost a lot of money!" In fact it was estimated to cost about £2,000.

Mr Hughes and his men drove away and made out their report: "The major portion of the arable land is foul and exceedingly poor; 8 acres of seeds is a fair plant; 6 acres planted with potatoes, swedes and cabbages have produced a medium crop, part of the oat stubble has been ploughed out; 4 acres of summer fallow has been planted with winter oats . . . The whole of the pasture land is poor, worn-out turf, very badly drained and covered with rushes in many places. It is not possible to plough it all out and reseed it." They concluded: "We consider that there will be no improvement under the existing management."

Ray was not shown the report. No written recommendations were ever sent and he was not offered any help in the form of labour. He was not noted for his tact and diplomacy. Like many farmers of his generation and upbringing he spoke his mind and he had made it clear that he was not going to spend any money on draining a field, especially as he did not own it. Marshy ground was a problem for the War Ag. There was a great deal of it all across the country, producing very little in the way of food. Land drainage was expensive and neither landlords, farmers nor the government could afford to finance it.

Bid's view of Camp Farm was quite different from that of Mr Hughes. She wrote, "Although we were life-long farmers we had had this farm for only three years and it was proving to be good, high-yielding and profitable land. The rent was economical and we were glad to be there."

Ray wondered if having so many horses on the farm had influenced the Warwickshire Committee against him. He knew that if he ploughed more he would not have sufficient grazing for the riding horses, let alone for the cattle.

However, on 4 August 1942 the Minister of Agriculture issued a directive to the Committees regarding horses. The minister appealed to horse owners to get rid of horses that were too old to work, or were kept for sentimental reasons. The directive added: "Care should of course be taken not to interfere with the retention of good horses that are capable of breeding and it should be borne in mind that with the growing restrictions on the use of petrol more horse traffic will be needed and this should be taken into account in deciding whether or not grassland should be ploughed up or used for the grazing of other animals."

One evening Bid said to me: "You know the War Ag. men came to see us recently, don't you?" I nodded. "Well, they want us to drain the Bog Field and plant it with wheat or potatoes." "But surely it would never grow anything like that!" I replied. "No," Bid agreed. "Well, I suppose it might if it were drained, but it would cost a lot more money than we've got to drain it properly and dredge the stream and do all that they say we must do."

"Then what'll happen?" "That's the trouble, we might have to leave." Leave! I was horror struck. "It was a land commissioner that came today and he confirmed the order to drain and plough it." In his private report Mr Hughes had written that it was not possible to drain it all but this opinion was not conveyed to Ray.

The land commissioner had actually told him that in view of the work and expense involved he would be a fool to do it. Ray replied "I don't need you to tell me that. I know." The amount of food that the field would grow would never be worth all the trouble and expense involved in draining it. It was a crazy command.

Ray discussed his situation with one or two other farmers he met at market. Until he spoke with others it had not occurred to him how open to corruption dealings with the War Ags. were. Suppose one of the Committee members had a son he wanted to keep out of the army. If the boy had a farm then he would be exempt from call-up. It was no problem to evict a farmer from his farm simply by reporting that he was a bad farmer or by giving the farmer some directive that he could not carry out. It constituted a wartime order, a command, direct from the Ministry of Agriculture; the farmer could not appeal to anyone, he had to vacate his farm, and the chosen tenant went into the farm. Ray did not know if there was anything like this in his particular case but it increased his resentment against the War Ag.

"But couldn't you raise the money somehow, Dad?" I pleaded. "There must be some way to get money for draining a field. Couldn't we borrow it?" "And throw it away!" he said. "What's the use of spending hundreds of pounds on a field like that? No. I'm not ploughing thirty acres of wet sod, and I'm not draining it, not for nobody!"

Was there no one to whom we could appeal against this unfairness? What about the National Farmer's Union? Ray had never had much time for them, and in any case some of the Union Committee members were also War Ag. Committee officials. He could have appealed back to the War Agricultural Executive Committee itself at its next meeting. He thought about going, but in the end he did not attend. He was afraid he would lose his temper and it was unlikely that he would have changed the Committee's mind.

When he did not attend the meeting on 17 November the minutes recorded: "It was resolved: that the Lands Officer be instructed to terminate the tenancy of Mr F.W. Raybould on 31 January 1943 . . . ". As some of the Camp Farm fields lay in Staffordshire that county's War Ag. was requested "to join in the Notice of Termination and Taking Possession".

Other farmers on the verge of dispossession went to appeal to Mr Hughes and the Warwickshire Committee but they were usually not successful. There was, for instance, Mr R.E. Phelps of Grange Farm, Balsall Common, who, like

~ THE KITCHEN ~

us, had been on his farm for only three years and was short of the necessary capital to carry out the orders. The Committee quizzed Mr Phelps when he went to appeal but Mr Hughes' final words were, "Well, Mr Phelps, the Committee have carefully discussed this case, and they are sorry to say that they have come to the decision that the appeal must fail and the order stand subject to the Minister's approval."

Mr Pratt of Chesford Poultry Farm was another who appeared before the Committee. He was incensed with his treatment by the Poultry Panel and had nearly come to blows with one of the inspectors. He tried to reason with Mr Hughes. He said, "My objection to this inspection was that these Members spent between seven and ten minutes upon which to inspect 3,000 head of poultry. They only handled one or two birds. Members of my staff remarked that it was a quick inspection." He pointed out that sending competitive people in business was unfair. He asked, "Who inspects their farms?" "Their farms are inspected by the panel," Mr Hughes replied. "They can't be if they are on the panel," Mr Pratt said. Mr Hughes did not comment on that. He and his Committee were deaf to any inferences of unfairness on the part of the War Ag. and refused to acknowledge that a poultry farmer competitor who went to inspect a similar business on behalf of the War Ag. could close it down at a word.

Mr Wilcox of Grove Farm, Chesterton, was another in grave trouble. He did not attend the meeting himself but sent a friend, Mr Margetts, who, when asked why Mr Wilcox had not come told Mr Hughes that "Mr Wilcox is only a farmer and would probably have died of fright." The tenants of the Estate and of the area in which the farm was situated had signed a letter to the effect that Mr Wilcox was a good farmer but this did not influence Mr Hughes in the least.

Mr Wilcox had 170 arable acres and had requested the loan of a Lister plough and a Fordson tractor from the War Ag. but the Committee had refused them. Mr Hughes had no comment to make on the subject. After some discussion, when it became clear that Mr Wilcox would have to give up his farm, Mr Margetts asked, on Mr Wilcox's behalf, if he could stay on longer so he could get his threshing done and sell his farm implements. He said, "He has nowhere to go and will have a hard job to find a place." Mr Hughes replied that Mr Wilcox had been fully warned and must face his responsibilities.

Ray and Bid decided to appeal to the Minister of Agriculture himself and sent a carefully composed letter to Mr Hudson but back came a reply saying that "no step had been taken by the Agricultural Committee without the full approval of the Minister". Mr Hudson was informed of each dispossession. Occasionally questions would be asked in the House of Commons. In July 1941 the case of Mr Mason of Malton in Yorkshire was discussed. One MP asked, "Was this farmer actually evicted from his home? Was he given the opportunity to continue work in some capacity upon the farm?" Mr Hudson replied, "He has certainly been evicted from the house because it is required for the new tenant. I do not know what he is going to do in the future."

Our hopes had been dashed by the reply to the letter. As another resort Ray wrote to the landlord of Camp Farm. Bid wrote, "The landlord, Lieut-Col. Manley, was away with the Army in the Middle East. His wife came to see us and said it would not have happened had he been at home, but nothing could be done, there was no one to appeal to for justice. The War Ag. was all powerful." I was later to learn that a landlord could not usually persuade the War Ag. to allow his tenant to stay on.

As for me, it seemed as if I were living in a story book. Soon I would turn to the last page and find that the heroine, along with her family and friends, would have won through to happiness. But, as time went by, there were no developments to back up my optimism that something would surely happen to save us from having to leave Camp Farm. Because I was a child I believed that what was fair would surely be recognised.

But then Ray and Bid gave up the fight to stay on. There was nothing more that they could do, no one else to whom they could make a protest. They were of a generation that accepted authority easily even when they did not agree with it, but there was, in fact, absolutely nothing more that they could have done with the system set up as it was. We were given two and a half months' notice to quit. In Wiltshire a Malmesbury man was given only one week.

Ray didn't whistle as he went about his work any more. Indeed he had no heart to bother much about the farm work and did only what was necessary for the welfare of the animals. Now and again he went off hunting on Mist with the South Staffordshire hounds which were still in operation, kept going by Mr Ryman. "I might as well enjoy myself while I can," Ray said glumly, and his hunting days did brighten that desperately gloomy November. He had the auction sale planned for 11 December when everything that we possessed, that we wouldn't need again, or could manage without, would be sold in the farmyard.

We didn't know where we would go, and had little money. We had no house to sell, no buildings, no land, for, of course, the farm was rented. The War Ags. paid no compensation to farmers that they dispossessed and no attempt was made to find them accommodation. Not one penny did Ray receive for the loss of his livelihood. We were as bereft as if our house had been hit by a bomb, for if we did not move out by 31 January the bailiffs would come and put us and our furniture out on the street. We were war casualties, with no accommodation, and Ray had no work.

At that time we were unacquainted with any other farmers who had also lost their farms through the War Ag. directives. Had we then known others in similar circumstances we would have realised that good fortune had not totally deserted us for we did, in the end, manage to find a roof over our heads. It was better to leave as gracefully as possible rather than wait for bailiffs and policemen to arrive and our furniture to be thrown into the lane. We eventually discovered that this happened to some people.

A year or two later Ray met Mr Griffin of Kings Coughton Farm, near Alcester, and his son, Tom. Mr Griffin's family had actually been evicted by the Warwickshire pest officer and had watched as the furniture was carried out of the house by bailiffs. They had nowhere to live. Mr Griffin and Tom took shelter in a disused hen-house while relations took in Mrs Griffin and the daughter, who was married to a serving soldier, and her children.

The tenant that the War Ag. had chosen for the Griffins' farm did not want the occupancy of the house and it remained vacant for six months even though the owner of it, Mr Griffin, was obliged to live in the hen-house in a nearby field, which he also owned. Then he was requested to remove the hut "from the Ministry's land", so Mr Griffin had to pay £300 for a plot in a neighbour's field. Mr Griffin was not at all clear in his mind as to why he had been dispossessed in the first place. His son, Tom, believed that it was because their farm was between two large estates whose owners did not like the fact that Mr Griffin could shoot any of their birds that happened to fly across his land.

Bid wrote, "Learning that there was a house to be sold not far from Redditch, Ray went to the auction hoping to get it, though I said to him 'What's the good of a house with no job?' But he would never consider working for another farmer, nor 'Digging for Victory' again. He was surprised to see my brother, Ernest, there. Of course, we had no telephones then. Ernest advised him not to make a bid for the house as there was a small house belonging to my mother which would be empty soon if we could just hang on for a week or two. It was a bit of luck for us, but unfortunate that an old lady had to die before we could have the house."

The worst day of all in that dreadful period, as far as I was concerned, was the day that Nellie went. I will never forget the last time I saw her. A lorry came to the farm, I don't remember what for, but Ray said to the driver, "Call her to you." Nellie went to the driver and he stroked her. He climbed into his cab and he took Nellie with him and he drove away. "Dad, Dad, where's Nell gone?" Ken and I cried. "To a new home," Ray said shortly, turning his back on us and marching off into the barn. I could tell he was upset.

Ken and I watched the lorry disappearing down the lane and began to wail. "Oh! you shouldn't have. Oh! get her back! Oh! No! Our Nellie!" In the house Bid's was the voice of reason. "She had to go. We couldn't take a dog like her to a tiny house in town. She wouldn't like to have been penned up.

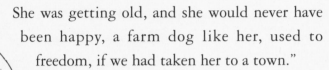

She was getting old, and she would never have been happy, a farm dog like her, used to freedom, if we had taken her to a town."

Oh! Nell, Dear Nell! She had shared so much with us: the golden summers of Enville, fetching the cows, rat hunting, rabbiting, her puppies, following in the fields through all the seasons. She was always there, interested in what was going on. How bewildered she would be! I cried and cried and felt so bad about Nellie.

Then there was Jock to be disposed of, but with him it was a little easier. It was arranged that Willy Giesen should take him. Willy had found another farm to take his caravan to and the farmer there had agreed to look after Jock during the week. I told Willy that as soon as we were able, when the war was over perhaps, and everything was normal, I would reclaim Jock.

On the day of the auction sale I was at school. I cycled home to an empty and silent farmyard. All had been taken away, everything from our old lawn mower, which sold for £1 and the car at £12 10 shillings, to the great Staffordshire harvest wagon, which had made only 14 shillings (70p) because no one really wanted such cumbersome vehicles any more. Ray was feeling bitter because one of the War Ag. men had attended and had bought his best hunter colt. After commission, Ray collected £689 on the sale of the farm stock and machinery with which to begin his new life.

Even Sandy, the fierce cat, was gone. Bid had been worrying as to what to do with him, but he decided his future for himself. He walked out at the time of the sale, never to return. No doubt he felt a sense of insecurity about the place. He had arrived when we had settled at Camp Farm, spent a part of his wild life with us until we were about to leave and then departed whence he came.

It was just before Christmas and it was a terrible time. We went to and fro in misery across the silent yard, where not so much as a chicken remained. In a daze we walked to fetch milk from a neighbouring farm. We did not know what to do with ourselves but were obliged to stay there until the old lady who lived in the house in Redditch died and we could move into it. We passed through the dead, non-event days like ghosts. On Christmas Day we children received, with no real joy, the simple presents that Bid had saved hard to buy. On Boxing Day we were invited to tea by one of the caravan families in their lovely house in Sutton Coldfield. We were all unnaturally subdued and quiet, and life seemed quite unreal.

It was a relief when the day to leave drew near. We did not relish the prospect of the little terraced house, but at least the gloom of the last few weeks and the sadness of our empty farm could be put behind us, even if it could never, ever, be forgotten.

The day before the removal van came to take us to Redditch Ray opened the back door in the morning and found a black kitten on the doorstep. Sympathetic neighbours must have left him there as a parting gift but we never knew who they were. We called him Lucky, and hoped indeed that he would bring us good fortune.

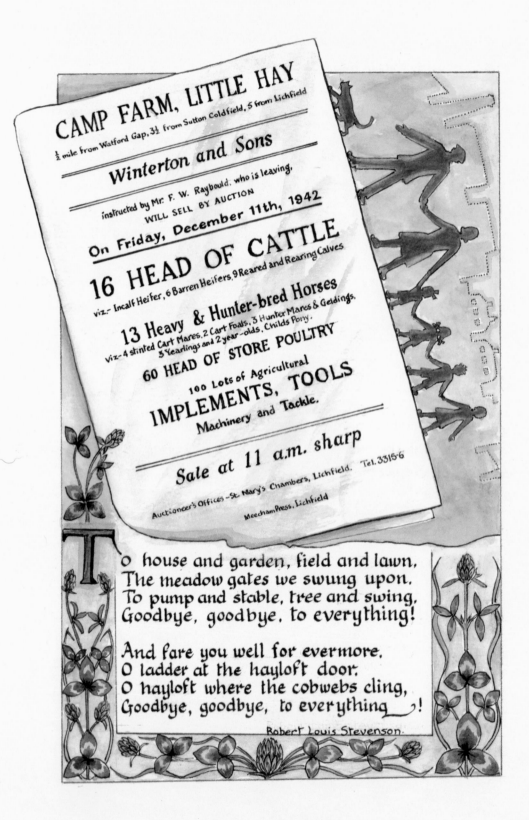

CAMP FARM, LITTLE HAY

½ mile from Watford Gap, 3½ from Sutton Coldfield, 5 from Lichfield

Winterton and Sons

instructed by Mr. F. W. Raybould, who is leaving,

WILL SELL BY AUCTION

On Friday, December 11th, 1942

16 HEAD OF CATTLE

viz:- Incalf Heifer, 6 Barren Heifers, 9 Reared and Rearing Calves

13 Heavy & Hunter-bred Horses

viz:- 4 stinted Cart Mares, 2 Cart Foals, 3 Hunter Mares & Geldings, 3 Yearlings and 2 year-olds, Childs Pony.

60 HEAD OF STORE POULTRY

100 Lots of Agricultural

IMPLEMENTS, TOOLS

Machinery and Tackle.

Sale at 11 a.m. sharp

Auctioneer's Offices—St. Mary's Chambers, Lichfield.   Tel. 3315·6

Meecham Press, Lichfield

T O house and garden, field and lawn,
The meadow gates we swung upon,
To pump and stable, tree and swing,
Goodbye, goodbye, to everything!

And fare you well for evermore,
O ladder at the hayloft door,
O hayloft where the cobwebs cling,
Goodbye, goodbye, to everything—!

Robert Louis Stevenson.

CHAPTER TEN

Cooped in Town

We lived now in a world where neighbours peeped from behind lace curtains, statuettes of Alsatian dogs or potted ferns guarded front windows from the passer-by's gaze and we could no longer scream and shout when we felt like it, for fear of disturbing our fellow townsfolk. Our house, 59 Grove Street, Redditch, had been built by Bid's grandfather. It was a red-brick Victorian end-of-terrace house, with a blue-brick entry along the side, dividing it from the next block of houses. At the rear there was a narrow yard, with a yellow privet hedge on one side taking up half its width and on the other side was the kitchen, coal hole and privy. From the front bay window we looked out over another privet hedge to the street, beyond which was a static water tank and the Scout Hut. Here, on Saturday nights the GIs came to dance and to flirt with the local girls. Bid wrote, "The house was substantial and dry, like all the houses my grandfather had built. The children had nowhere to play compared with the acres they had enjoyed previously and their ball 'always bounced onto someone else's land'."

Judith and Lucky at 59, Grove Street Redditch

We were caged as wild birds. Ken stood on the back door step surveying the blue-brick yard. "Well, exactly just how far does our land go to?" he enquired. Bid remembered, "The first night we were in bed there Ray and I laughed together when hearing footsteps, or a pedestrian whistling, along the pavement below our bedroom window. We weren't in the country now!"

It was a novelty and a luxury to have the shops so close at hand, school only a few hundred yards away, and relations on Bid's side of the family living nearby, but these, even in a small way, were no compensation for the way of life we had lost. I escaped at every opportunity to the Abbey Meadows on the outskirts of the town where grassy mounds concealed mysterious ancient ruins and the River Arrow flowed sweetly under the alders. On my bicycle I explored narrow Roman Icknield Street and the lanes around Beoley. In summer Christine and I climbed out through a bedroom window on to the sloping roof of the kitchen, and lay spread-eagled upon the slates trying to catch the the rays of the sun, until Bid told us to come down before we broke our necks.

Ray soon found a job. Bid wrote, "Fortunately, Mabel's husband was able to get work for Ray in a factory foundry. The war continued and aeroplane parts were in constant demand. Ray had never been afraid of work, thanks to his father's training, but when he sometimes worked through the night and I was alone for the first time in my life, I thought how different it was from walking up and down a furrow, ploughing in the fresh air, with horses and dog, and probably a child. I noticed the healthy glow disappear from his cheeks and the sparkle from his eye, and the general alertness gradually vanish with this new life and the night work, for which the upgraded income would never compensate."

Knowing nothing else but farming he became a labourer in the aluminium foundry of the High Duty Alloys. All over town you could hear the occasional dull thud as its "big hammer" dropped. It sounded a fearful place and at first Ray found it to be so. It was filthy, with searing heat from the molten metal and the deafening roar of the furnaces. To the regular workers Ray probably seemed a simple soul, they played no end of tricks on him which he always took in good part. In his time he had met some rough men: cattle drovers, gypsies, casual labourers on the farm, but the foundrymen were rougher than all of them. They used foul language such as he had never heard even in the cattle markets, but he learned to endure it all, accept his pay packet with thanks, the meanwhile making plans as to what to do next.

He arrived home each day grimed with metallic, sooty dirt, not fresh smelling like newly ploughed soil or even natural, like cow muck. He was often bad-tempered and tired, especially when he was on night shift. During his farming life he had only been up in the night for air raids and difficult calvings. Cycling home from work on a beautiful summer morning and

In the 1940's Redditch was a town of less than 30,000 people. It was world famous for NEEDLES of all kinds, FISH HOOKS and FISHING TACKLE and SPRINGS.

MILWARDS SPECIAL SCHOOL NEEDLES No. 4

JOHN JAMES & SONS REDDITCH
CELEBRATED EGG EYED SHARP 6/10 PATENTED

CRESCENT PIN STU

ALFRED SHRIMPTON & SONS TRADE MARK

needle dispenser from the firm Bid worked for in the 1920's

REDDITCH
the river Arrow flows nearby

a needle-making town from the early 1700's

having to go home to a darkened room to sleep was more than he could face, so sometimes he would walk up to the hills behind the factory and sleep in the fields under a hedge.

Arriving home from school one afternoon I found him writing a letter. This was uncharacteristic. Usually he persuaded Bid to write his letters because his spelling was so poor. "What's he doing?" I asked Bid. She passed me the latest copy of *Farmer and Stockbreeder* which Ray had bought on his way home from work. In it was a small advertisement asking for dispossessed farmers to write to a Major Bowron in Rickmansworth, Herts. Ray signed his letter with a flourish, passed it over to Bid for checking, then rushed out to post it. "It's too late," Bid said. "What can anyone do about it now? They can't give the farms back to us."

Eventually a note came back. A meeting was called at The Friends' Meeting House, in Euston, London. Ray donned his best suit and caught the train for Euston, leaving us to speculate as to how many would turn up and whether anything could be done for us. It was late when he climbed the hill home from the station. Yes, it had been worth going, he said. He thought there were about two hundred there and most of them had lost their farms. "By God! There was something said, I can tell you!" he exclaimed. It seemed that emotions, tempers and voices had risen high indeed. Disgust with the War Ag. men knew no limits. "Corruption! I'm not the only one as thinks some farms have been handed to friends of the War Ag. men. There's plenty others as thinks the same! And compensation! Nobody there had had a penny. We're lucky, I can tell you. You should hear what happened to some of them. Put out on the street, living in old shacks, because they had nowhere else to go. And one was shot! Shot to death!"

Amid an uproar the Major had called the meeting to order and a committee was formed, a difficult operation since none of the farmers, who came from all parts of the country, were known to one another. They decided to call themselves The Dispossessed Farmers' and Supporters' Association and one of their most important aims was to fight for the right of appeal in the Law Courts before independent judges who were not connected with the War Agricultural Executive Committees.

Perhaps it was not surprising when the next meeting was held in the same place that the treasurer, who had volunteered for the position, was conspicuous by his absence. Neither he nor the one guinea subscriptions he had collected were ever seen again. "Of course," said Ray, when he arrived home after that meeting, "some of them were saying that the treasurer was planted on us by the War Ag. itself, with the aim of discouraging us. There were a lot there as cried 'Sabotage!', when he didn't show up, I can tell you." He went on, "We're going on with it all, though. We paid again. We've got a new treasurer. He's all right. Looks genuine." "Well, I should just hope so!" Bid said. Soon she was busy helping the cause, addressing envelopes and sending off leaflets to destinations all over the country.

At about the same time as the farmers were setting up this nationwide association there was, in Essex, a separate society being formed, which called itself the Essex Farmers' and Countrymans' Association, based at Peldon Rectory. Several meetings were held, composed of people who were unhappy with their treatment from the Essex War Ag. and there was a considerable amount of publicity given to their grievances in the press. According to the writer J. Wentworth Day, this resulted in a visit to Peldon from Mr Hudson himself, and soon afterwards matters there improved considerably. The Essex Association was therefore short-lived as further evictions were prevented.

Some counties' War Ags. were more dictatorial than others. Essex was one of these, Warwickshire was another, yet all the counties seemed to have their dispossessions. Up in Northumberland 67-year-old Mr George Bell, whose son normally helped him on the farm but had been called up into the Cameron Highlanders, was given notice to quit. Alone, he could not carry out all the War Ag. directives. He and his wife moved into a nearby cottage and the farm was advertised to let. While his wife was showing a prospective tenant round his farm the depressed Mr Bell shot himself. Afterwards local farmers offered to help Mrs Bell with labour and implements to keep the farm going until the son came home but the War Ag. would not permit this.

— Wiltshire Down Sheep —

Ray looked forward to the farmers' meetings in London. They were almost as good as Shrewsbury horse sales. It took his mind away, temporarily, from the roaring furnaces at the High Duty Alloys. He could gossip with kindred spirits who knew what the seasons of the year stood for in terms of proper work. They settled on the name "The Farmers' Rights Association" and a solicitor, Mr L.V. Priestley, became both treasurer and secretary. He had been a lawyer in London, but, as a conscientious objector, he had moved to a farm in Cardington, Shropshire, and set up his practice in Church Stretton. He was the kind of man who took up deserving causes and although he had had no problems with his own farm he felt that the dispossessed farmers had been treated very unfairly. The President was Sir Walter Blount of Sodington Hall at Mamble in Worcestershire.

Ray always sat with the same group of men who had been seated next to him at the very first meeting and they became life-long friends. There was Walter Powell, a bachelor in late middle age who had owned his farm since 1912. On his six hundred acres near Marlborough in Wiltshire he kept

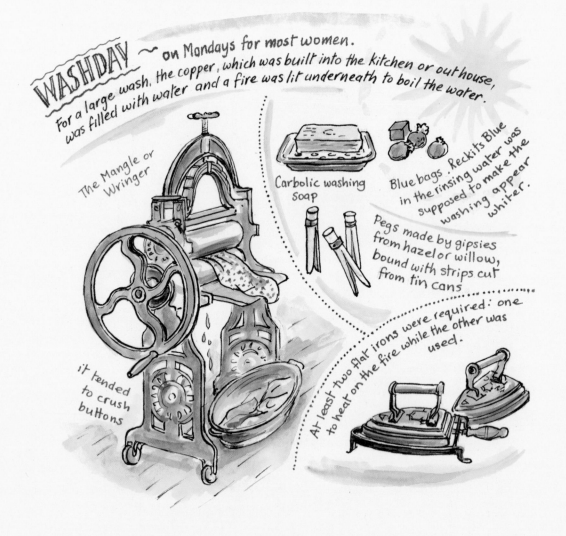

WASHDAY ~ on Mondays for most women.
For a large wash, the copper, which was built into the kitchen or out house, was filled with water and a fire was lit underneath to boil the water.

The Mangle or Wringer

it tended to crush buttons

Carbolic washing soap

Blue bags. Reckits Blue in the rinsing water was supposed to make the washing appear whiter.

Pegs made by gipsies from hazel or willow, bound with strips cut from tin cans

At least two flat irons were required: one to heat on the fire while the other was used.

between one and two hundred pigs, about twenty-five milking cows and other cattle, six working horses and five hundred sheep. The War Ag. ordered him to plough fifty acres of grass and plant it with oats, but his farm was isolated in the rolling Wiltshire Downs and he could not find the labour to do the work. He asked for the War Ag. to supply labour and officers visited him to discuss his difficulties. The Land Commissioner told him that he would be assisted, but then, a week later, he received notice to quit in five weeks.

Another who became a good friend was Herbert Markham. He had been a tenant farmer of one hundred and fifty acres near Towcester in Northamptonshire. He was a sheep man. On his grassland he ran two hundred and twenty sheep as well as twenty-three cattle, he had about fifty acres of grain and grew a small amount of flax and kale. Like so many others he did not have sufficient capital to please the War Ag. who wanted him to invest more in the rented farm. Although his neighbours wrote to the Northampton Committee supporting his contention that he had made considerable improvement to the farm since he had taken it over four years before when it had been extremely run down, these letters did not sway the Committee when he went along to appeal. His tenancy was terminated in May 1942.

He, his wife and four children lived for a while in a condemned cottage while he worked in an aeroplane factory but when Ray met him the tide had turned for him. He was working for the Forestry Commission in North Wales and the tenancy of a small hill farm came with the job. He was a jolly man with a smooth pink complexion and crinkly fair hair. He wrote to say that if we wanted a bit of country life again we should go to him for a holiday. We gratefully accepted. "When we get into their rick yard," Christine said with great anticipation, "we can just stand and scream and scream!" So upon the slopes of Hafod Owen she and the other two let off steam. Their screams of freedom echoed round the Welsh mountains at the first opportunity and no one told them to be quiet.

That visit introduced us to the mountains, to tiny plants of sundew and butterwort in bogs, to wild goats, to carrying hay on a horse-drawn sled on the steep fields, to postmen who delivered letters by horseback and to wonderfully clever sheep dogs. Bid and Mrs Markham became firm friends and we were to visit the family many times in the future.

On his bicycle Ray went out to call on other farmers near Redditch to see if he could persuade them to become members of the Association. He visited Mr Griffin in his hut at Alcester and his son, Tom Griffin, sometimes accompanied Ray when he called on others. Most farmers were fearful of joining the Association. They thought that if they did then the

War Ag. might mark them down for dispossession as well. Ray went to see Mr Oliver Aldington who had refused to plough a large boggy area on his Lower House Farm at Mappleborough Green. He had been forced to sell up and to move with his wife and daughter to a small house in Redditch.

Despite Ray having little success in persuading the farmers round about to join the Association the numbers countrywide who became members steadily grew to about five thousand. It was difficult in wartime to obtain publicity. Occasionally the farming magazines would print a column on disputes and dispossessions in places which ranged from Merioneth to Suffolk, including one where the Rutland War Ag. was compulsorily acquiring land after a man had been in possession of it for only nineteen days! The Association itself produced a booklet citing twenty-three cases taken from its files and with an introduction which enquired as to what the average townsman would say if he were dismissed from his job and evicted from his home on to the street with no accommodation provided, all without any trial or compensation.

There was Mr D. Hildreth of Gravel Pit Farm, Towthorpe, Yorkshire, who had taken on the derelict farm in 1939 after it had been empty for two years. It was in such a bad condition that he had paid no rent for the first year, but after only three years there and never having refused a War Ag. order, he was turned out.

Mr Meredith Hunt, of the two hundred and twelve acre Empshill Farm, at Farmington in Gloucestershire did not know the reason for his dispossession. He said he had never refused an order and when he moved out of the house a War Ag. member moved into it. Likewise, the brother of a War Ag. member moved into Lodge Farm, Gowdall, Goole in Yorkshire, when farmer J. Jackson, who had not previously received any complaint, was forced to move out.

At Ash House Farm, Great Wolford, Warwickshire, Mr R.S. Mitchell was asked to lay out £2,000 to make improvements on a farm he rented. He was not willing to do this and to his complete surprise he was told by the War

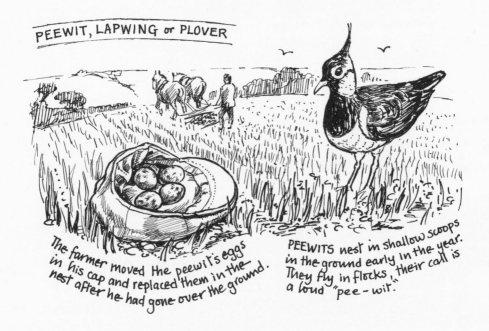

PEEWIT, LAPWING or PLOVER

The farmer moved the peewit's eggs in his cap and replaced them in the nest after he had gone over the ground.

PEEWITS nest in shallow scoops in the ground early in the year. They fly in flocks, their call is a loud "pee-wit."

Ag. member that he would have to ask his committee to terminate the tenancy.

Some Members of Parliament felt that the system was very wrong. It was reported that in Cockermouth, Cumbria, "Colonel Alan Dower MP Hits out at Un-English Methods". He criticised the power of the War Ag. He said, "The right of appeal has always been exercised by Englishmen ever since the Norman Conquest."

In the national newspapers two or three articles appeared but brought forth no reponse from the government. All the same, members of the Association did not give up hope of obtaining compensation for dispossession and disturbance and for the right of appeal in court. They organised meetings in village halls to try to publicise their aims and to attract new members.

Bid remembered one meeting that she and Ray had attended: "In the village of Blockley in the Cotswolds, there was a particularly large gathering of country people, and as at most meetings of such nature, some were for the cause and some were against it. The vice-chairman made an embittered speech about the way some local farming families had been ordered to quit, stressing that there was nothing they could at present do about it. Everything was quite legal, according to the National Farmers' Union and the Ministry of Agriculture, which, in his anger, the speaker likened to the Gestapo. He even held up a large poster depicting a black swastika. But he had gone too far for at this there were cries of 'Boo' and 'Shame', and then 'Burn it!' Someone threw a box of matches, whereupon Mr Westwood set fire to a corner of it and we watched it shrivel up. If it did nothing else, the incident caused the meeting to be reported in the local press and thereby advertised the movement."

One weekend Ray made the journey back to Camp Farm specifically to see what the War Ag. and the new tenant, who had been a neighbour, had made of the Bog Field. When he leaned over the gate he felt both sad and triumphant for the field looked much as it always had done. Down by the road bridge over the stream some drainage pipes were strewn about amongst the rushes and a few ditches had been dug but they were now neglected. It was obvious that it had all been given up as a bad job. We had been dispossessed for nothing!

The Association lightened our days in that gloomy little house in Redditch and gave us hope, but I was impatient. "Why can't they get Camp Farm back for us?" That was what I wanted. "I don't see how they can," Bid replied. "Be practical. And just think how much it would cost us to start up again, all the new equipment and everything, and the animals." "Well, you did it once," I said, but I could tell that the spirit had gone out of them as far as farming was concerned. Starting again from scratch would be too much for them after everything that had happened.

The farmers of the Association did derive some satisfaction from a blackmail case which was brought before open court in Hampshire. It concerned a farm which had actually been bought by Mr Hudson himself, and the farmer who had sold it. During the proceedings it became quite clear that the War Ag. officials, and one of them in particular, had acted on several occasions in an untruthful, disgraceful and malicious manner.

The Judge did not hesitate to say so in his summing up. The case revealed a great many wrongdoings by the War Ag. but it was not widely reported. Ray said: "Ah! It will all come out in time. You'll see if it don't!"

Yet in 1945 Mr Hudson, when questioned in the House of Commons, declared that he had not heard of any case of hardship amongst the dispossessed farmers. In the light of the fact that some had committed suicide and others had no decent accommodation, this was an amazing statement.

The war finally came to an end. On 8 May 1945 it was VE Day, Victory in Europe Day. I celebrated at the fair with my girl friends. Ken, Christine and Judith went to a party in the Scout Hut across the road. They were town children now, playing in the street, throwing stones into the static water tank and spending halfpennies on liquorice sticks at the corner shop. Being younger than I was they did not remember the farm as clearly as I did.

Meanwhile Ray had been making plans to leave the foundry. "I don't know what to tell them at work," he said. "They want to make me a shop steward."

AFTER THE WAR

BREAD was not rationed during the war, but it was rationed from 1946-48. MEAT stayed rationed until 1951

The winter of 1946-7 was long and severe. Fuel of all kinds was scarce

The WOMENS' LAND ARMY, which reached its peak numbers in 1943 was disbanded in 1950. It never received the same recognition from the government as the other womens' forces.

More tractors began to appear on the fields. They had hydraulic power lift and implements could be hydraulically operated.

Italian Prisoners of War were sent from camps to work on farms (a few from 1941) and some were employed around Redditch until repatriated

During the petrol shortage, ponies and traps were in great demand.

With my friend Barbara who bought a trap to use with her pony, Star.

He thought it rather a joke for it was not a position he looked for. Trade Unions were not his style. "I shall have to let on soon that I'm leaving, shan't I?" He had decided to spend his small savings on a lock-up shop where he could sell boots and shoes. "I shall specialise in riding boots and shoes for country wear," he declared.

Houses were, after the war, very difficult to buy or to rent. There was hardly any accommodation available and newly married couples were usually obliged to live with parents. There seemed to be little chance that we could escape from Grove Street for several years but once the shoe shop was set up Bid had the idea of advertising for a country house to swap for a town house, and she was lucky. An elderly couple called, saying that they lived at Astwood Bank, a village high on a ridge, about three miles to the south of Redditch, and they wanted to live closer to town.

We liked their house, a red-brick Victorian villa, with a two-storeyed outhouse and small garden. There was open country just a couple of streets away and this we craved. We could not believe that the couple actually liked our terraced house, but they did. With some cash adjustment the swap was made.

Worcestershire terms:
"BOB OWLER" — a large furry moth.
DODDINS — small, sweet, green apples.

CHAPTER ELEVEN

A Village Home

Astwood Bank was a village of red-brick houses which often had attached buildings where outworkers kept small machines to carry out various tasks for needle and fishing tackle manufacture. The village was high on a ridge with pretty Worcestershire countryside falling away on either side. There were footpaths through meadows of wild flowers and woods that had long ago been part of the Forest of Feckenham. There were tall elms and old apple trees in gardens and westwards, across miles of chequered fields, the Malvern Hills changed in colour through the weather and the days.

"Perhaps we could have Jock back again," Bid suggested. The remark shocked me. Jock was from another world, another life. Could he still exist? He would be an old dog now! I couldn't bear to think of him. I didn't want to know what had happened to him. It was all too painful to think about those days, and dogs broke one's heart so! A schoolfriend had heard of a farm where there were puppies for sale and we cycled there, returning home with a ginger and white collie pup, carried back in a bicycle saddle bag. We called him Shandy and he

A SECRET JOY

We who were born
In country places
Far from cities
And shifting faces,
We have a birthright
No man can sell
And a secret joy
No man can tell.

For we are kindred
To lordly things,
The wild duck's flight
And the white owl's wings,
To pike and salmon,
To bull and horse,
The curlew's cry
And the smell of gorse.

Pride of trees,
Swiftness of streams,
Magic of frost
Have shaped our dreams;
No baser vision
Their spirit fills
Who walk by right
On the naked hills.

Charles Morgan (?)

Christine and Ken with
Shandy at Astwood Bank.

became a dearly beloved family dog.

Ray bought some Indian Game bantams and penned them behind wire netting in a corner of the garden. The little hens with their tiny eggs and the arrogant cockerel helped us to feel like country people again. Judith kept white mice who got lost in the coal shed and emerged as black ones. The family was getting back on an even keel and normality was returning.

Ray bought a strange looking three-wheeler van in which he drove to his shop, delivered boots and shoes, collected payments on a weekly round of customers and travelled about the country to see his farming friends. He helped them out at haymaking and harvest until the time came when skilled stookers of corn and builders of ricks were no longer needed and machines took over the labour of men and horses.

Once in a while we visited Egg Hill, but there were changes there. First Quintin married and he and his wife went to farm near Chirk. Then, in December 1947 Harold died. "Poor Harold hadn't been right for a year or so, not since the time when the horses bolted," Grandma said. "What horses were those, then, Grandma?" "The horses at Kings Norton station, my dear. Dragged near half a mile along the line he was," she replied. "Yet Harold was always so strong," Grandpa said. "I've seen him lift a sack of wheat as easy as a sack of feathers, many a time." "He was exhausted when he come home that day," Grandma went on. "I never saw him looking so white as on that day."

Harold had gone to the station to collect a pair of new horses. He asked the guard not to blow the whistle until he had taken the horses well clear of the train, but unfortunately the whistle had been blown too soon and they had bolted. Harold managed to hang on to them but had been dragged for a long distance.

Then, fifteen months later, Grandpa died at the age of seventy-eight. That left only Grandma and Bob at the farm as the other son, George, was in business on his own account. Before long Grandma and Bob sold up, ending over fifty years of hard family effort upon the Frankley land.

The Farmers' Rights Association continued for a while but it was losing momentum, until the day came when Ray announced that it was going to be disbanded. I felt sad for it represented the last link with our farming days. Everyone had been so hopeful at the beginning, but in reality very little had been achieved.

When the war ended those dispossessed farmers who had owned their farms had their homes and land returned to them. Unfortunately for tenant farmers their farms were gone forever as they were now occupied by others. At the end of the war a Labour government was elected and the Minister of Agriculture, Tom Williams, made many changes. Just as the right to appeal to an independent court had been restored after the First World War, so it was again restored now, but this did not apply in retrospect to those who had been dispossessed during the war and the question of compensation was not considered.

A great many families who lost their farms were left to spend the rest of their lives with a sense of stigma and shame. They did not talk about their experiences for fear people would think they had not co-operated to do their share to help in the war effort. No doubt there had been bad farmers but with no right of appeal this was unproven. It was all too complicated to explain that it had not always been possible to carry out orders, and that the War Ag. itself was not always as honest as it should have been. Misdemeanours and malpractices were all hushed up and no one mentioned dispossessions any more.

The official figures for the number of tenancies that were terminated between 1940 and 1945 was 2,742. The number of owner-occupiers who were evicted from their properties was said to be a far greater number and while many of these did return to their farms after the war was over, many others sold up in despair.

CHAPTER TWELVE

Leaning over the Gate

Once in a while, if I found myself anywhere near Lichfield, I would return to look at Camp Farm, just to lean over the gate for a little while and to note the changes. At first both the farm and the Bog Field looked much as they always had done. The field was a grassy expanse laced with flowers and rushes and there was obviously a farming family in the house. It all appeared to be more or less as we had left it.

I did not visit it again for many more years. By then the countryside all over England had begun to alter. Myxomatosis saw off millions of rabbits in the 1950s, and then all the elm trees died. Selective weedkillers, insecticides, fungicides and various chemicals were used on the crops, poisoning wildlife of all kinds. There were far fewer flowers, insects and birds. Their habitats were further reduced when thousands of miles of hedgerows were torn out to create larger fields for the massive machines which now cultivated the land.

An abandoned Threshing Machine.

Flush with the pond the lurid furnace burned
At eve, while smoke and vapour filled the yard;
The gloomy winter sky was dimly starred,
The fly-wheel with a mellow murmer turned;

While, ever rising on its mystic stair
In the dim light, from secret chambers borne,
The straw of harvest, severed from the corn,
Climbed and fell over, in the murky air.

Charles Tennyson Turner 1808-1879

With the increase in the numbers of tractors and the coming of the huge machines which could carry out all manner of different tasks, the heavy horses, which had constituted such an important part of country life, were becoming rare after about 1947. By the mid-1960s the Shire Horse was almost an extinct species and numbers of other heavy breeds were very low. These horses had taken many years of careful breeding to evolve.

The heavy horses were not the only familiar animals to disappear from the fields. Many of the old breeds of animals were going, too. Certain pig breeds all but died out, some kinds of sheep became scarce and the ubiquitous Shorthorn cattle almost vanished. Where some of these animals had been dual-purpose, now new breeds from other countries became fashionable because they gave more milk or leaner meat. Black and white Friesians and Holsteins replaced the Shorthorns while Limousins and Charolais were introduced for beef. Nowadays there was hardly ever a human being to be seen, laying a hedge, digging a ditch or hoeing a crop, and willing to pass the time of day with a passer-by.

The Bog Field could not escape the innovations. In the 1970s the old hawthorn bushes were pulled out, the willows and alders vanished from beside the stream and the stream itself was reduced to a deep culvert. The Bog Field was drained at last and it became a prairie of wheat just as the War Ag. had wanted it to be nearly forty years before.

The house and buildings underwent changes, too. With a small amount of land they were split off from the majority of the acres that Ray had rented. Silver birches grew upon the front lawn, the outhouse where Bid had done her mangling was taken down but instead there was a glass fronted porch displaying masses of rosettes and ribbons, no doubt won by the riding horses that nodded over loose-box doors and even peered out of the cow shed. I approved of that. It was strange and peculiar to return to the farm. It was sad, and yet I did not know why it should be so.

A few years later an incongruous new house appeared on the front lawn and the old house looked forlorn, part of it serving as a garage. I thought of all the people who had been grateful for shelter inside it during the air raids.

The property grew more and more run down and was finally bought by a builder who began to transform the old place out of all recognition. I was delighted to see that down beyond the stream someone had planted a thicket of alders.

Leaning over the Bog Field gate and surveying its modern aspect I can still see in my mind's eye Ray turning out the horses, the pony, Tommy, following closely on Mist's heels, and Nell chasing a rabbit through the lady's smocks. I can see us children paddling in the stream in summer, Christine falling into it, and I can hear cart wheels and horses' hooves crunching over the pebbles at the ford. What a host of memories there are contained in just one field! There was the man who periodically came to cut watercress and the gipsy family that Ray permitted to pitch a bender tent against the hedge, until he discovered that, one by one, our chickens were disappearing.

For the duration of all his eighty-nine years Ray never lost the look of a countryman. He was unmistakable in his old tweed jacket, crumpled trousers, battered hat and muddy shoes, always looking as if he had come straight from a cattle market. He would critically inspect someone's crop over a gate: a green and even crop, sown by huge drills drawn by tractors and sprayed against weeds and insects. Ray identified with the heavy horses and the Shorthorn cows. Farmers like him were almost all gone. It was all very different from farming in his time, and the countryside was altered, too.

Yet there were still views to stir the heart. "How can anybody die when there are sights like that to be seen!" he exclaimed one day as a covey of partridges suddenly whirred up at the edge of a wood.

Our days at Camp Farm are long past and the efforts of the farmers to obtain justice never did come to much. Those dispossessed by the War Ag. are forgotten now by almost everyone. Most of the farmers themselves have gone. Bid died in 1983 and Ray in 1989. Only a few of the children can remember. Yet we, in our small way, occupy a niche in the history of rural England.

Bibliography

SOURCES:

National Farm Survey, Public Record Office, MAF 32/965/Pt1 and others

War Agricultural Executive Committee Minutes, Public Record Office, MAF 80/907, 908, 1964, 2921 to
    2929, 2931, 2932, 2535, 3366, 3367

Manley Hall Estate Papers, Stafford Record Office

ARTICLES AND NEWSPAPERS:

'The Itchen Stoke Shooting Tragedy', *Hampshire Chronicle*, 3 August 1940, and the *Daily Mirror*, 24 July 1940

'Do They Call This Justice?', John Ridley, *Sunday Pictorial*, 27 June 1943

'They Broke a Widow's Heart', John Ridley, *Sunday Pictorial*, 17 October 1943

Farmers' Weekly, 4 July 1941, 10 November; 8 & 15 December 1944, 5 January 1945

Farmer and Stockbreeder, 15 December 1942, 31 August 1943

The Field, 13 January 1945, 17 & 24 February 1945

Judgment: Odlum v. Stratton. Reprinted by the *Wiltshire Gazette* late 1944(?)

'Living Casualties (The Dispossessed Farmer)' and 'The New Morality', *The Farmers' Rights Association*,
    undated, *c.* 1946–8

BOOKS:

Chivers, Keith, *The Shire Horse* (J.A. Allen & Co.,1976)

Dakers, Caroline, *The Countryside at War 1914–18* (Constable, 1987)

Dewey, P.E., *British Agriculture in the First World War* (Routledge, 1989)

Ernle, Lord, *English Farming Past and Present* (Longman, Green & Co., 1936)

Fream, W, *Fream's Elements of Agriculture*, 8th edn (John Murray, 1918)

Henderson, G., *The Farming Ladder* (Faber & Faber, 1943)

Hennell, Thomas, *Change in The Farm* (Cambridge University Press, 1934)

Hurd, Anthony, *A Farmer in Whitehall* (Country Life, 1951)

Murray, K.A.H., *History of the Second World War: Agriculture* (HMSO & Longman, Green & Co., 1955)

Raybould, Marion Isabel, 'Memoirs' (unpublished) (1974)

Ward, Sadie, *War in the Countryside,1939–1945* (David & Charles, 1988)

Wentworth Day, J., *Harvest Adventure* (Harrap & Co. Ltd, 1946)